MW01033469

The Everyday Leader

Masterfully Lead the People Who MUST Report to You

Real stories and actionable strategies to reduce missteps and grow in people leadership

Lindiwe Stovall Lester

P.S.E. Institute, 2022

The Everyday Leader, Masterfully Lead the People Who MUST Report to You

First edition. First printing 2022.

ISBN number: 978-1-7344826-2-1

Library of Congress Cataloguing-in-Publication Data

Lester, Lindiwe S.

The Everyday Leader, masterfully lead the people who MUST report to you

- Business Management
- Personal Development
- Team Development
- Workplace Culture
- Leadership Coaching
- Interpersonal Relationships

Dedicated to my late father, Willie Stovall Jr.,

a leader for as long as I can remember,

and in his own way.

The Everyday Leader

Contents

Keep *The Everyday Leader* handy for ongoing use. Review the chapter titles to go directly to what you need when you need it.

Real stories are dispersed through the book to help make the content come alive for you. Names have been omitted or changed, except where specific permission was given.

Visuals: Charts, Models, Key Concepts

Page

Introduction

Framing the Conversation

"I throw up every day on my train ride to work."

"I only view one of my five supervisors as a great manager."

"My supervisor's coaching helped me do my job better; it also made a big difference in how I relate to my teenagers."

"My business would be so much better if I could clone myself, rather than have to keep firing the people I get."

"I lose sleep just thinking about going to board meetings."

These five remarks are real; they were shared with me. They are illustrative of the many comments that inspire me to partner with leaders as they strive to enhance their underdeveloped *people* skills. Though it's common for leaders to be blinded to their growth needs, it comes at a cost. This inattention can have unintended and harmful effects on those who report to them and on the organization. Meanwhile, these leaders remain obliviously mired in a state of underachievement.

All but one of the opening remarks are less than desirable, and neither of those four scenarios has to be the case at work, on teams, or in volunteer groups. Leaders can be better, and those in their charge can thrive when that happens.

The Emergence of the Book

What if Gallup is right?

This question has nagged me over the last several years. When I'd take breaks from writing or question *why* I'm writing this book with so many others available, Gallup's disconcerting data kept returning me to this undertaking. It's critical, because Gallup and others suggest leaders are leaving a lasting, and often devastating, effect on a lot of people in their wakes.

I began writing *The Everyday Leader* in 2017, chronicling decades of leading others and consulting—efforts directed towards facilitating individual growth and mindset change. I wanted to understand which factors contributed to that growth and which leader practices appeared as recurring themes that inclined leaders to falter. Gallup's 2015 *State of the American Manager* report and their 2017 study on the American workplace cemented my resolve to publish *The Everyday Leader*. **These Gallup reports maintain that only 10% of the workforce have the talent to manage people.** I thought: **What if Gallup is right?** Do the calculation. If they're correct, a full 90% of the people in the workplace should *not* be supervising workmates.

After reviewing their findings, the challenge became clearer and more manageable. The authors explained that though only 10% of the workforce are well-suited to supervise others, only 10% of the workforce *need* to occupy these roles. The problem is that those who are in the manager roles are typically not the 10% with the attributes for those best suited for those roles.

Research indicates those who should lead others aren't in the roles, and those who shouldn't, are.

Are most of us in these *people-leader* positions fomenting distress (to greater or lesser degrees) for those who have no choice but to report to us? I resolved to examine how those given the leadership mantle can do better for the people who have little choice but to follow us.

It's apparent, based on Gallup's findings, that the way forward is two-fold: 1) better identify and expand the ranks of those well-suited for leading teams of people, and 2) strengthen the competencies of those already in these leader roles. *The Everyday Leader* supports these two imperatives.

The skillset for attracting, retaining, developing and inspiring *people for high performance* is neither common nor innate. To develop the attributes for effectiveness *requires* leaders spend more time looking *inward* at our own need to grow, and less *outward* seeking who or what to blame when falling short.

This book is singularly focused on supporting leaders in getting the best from the PEOPLE they directly supervise and lead. Whether paid or unpaid, in business or community, leaders are affecting people every day and everywhere. I'm confident that each *people leader* will glean at least a few ideas and tools from the book to build their skills to inspire people to do their best work in service to their organization's goals.

Leaders thrive when they develop or at least brush up on their *people* skills.

Who Am I to Write This Book?

For 40 years, I've worked as a leader and with leaders, in large and small nonprofits, with entrepreneurs, and community organizations. *The Everyday Leader* draws from that store of experiences what's most notable and beneficial for growth-oriented leaders.

I've been a strategic partner to new leaders, tenured leaders, emerging leaders, multi-cultural leaders, teen leaders, and leaders who are more suited to being stellar individual contributors (i.e., *supervising no one*). I've held positions endowed with no positional authority. These required me to be increasingly more effective with people—whether leading mentoring groups or leading strategy, diversity and community development learning cohorts. There were situations where, despite many efforts, I was unable to bring the disparate personalities together to get anything done. I learned from these as well.

I've studied assessment models as one approach to help direct reports and clients observe and leverage their styles and strengths, then explore growth opportunities. According to DISC®, I'm behaviorally a combination of the Influence and Dominant styles; Myers-Briggs says I'm ENTJ (Extraversion, iNTuitive, Thinking, Judging); Strength Finders repeatedly shows my top five strengths as Strategic, Achiever, Learner, Connectedness, and Input.

As a *Learner*, I've continued to sharpen my people development competencies. For decades I've been drawn to such themes as social and emotional intelligence, strengths-based leadership, optimizing the performance environment (and aligning culture), coaching and feedback, systems thinking, facilitating team development, and strategic leadership. Two *people* development-related graduate degrees along with certifications in coaching, facilitation, and evaluation hopefully lend credibility to the book's content.

I've amassed lots of notes, developed tools, plans, processes, and learning interventions. I've also tracked action plans and progress of direct reports and clients to observe how growth happens and what stifles it.

From the perspective of both leading and being led (supervised), I posed questions to nonprofit CEOs, C-suite executives, entrepreneurs, young supervisors, and HR professionals. These human voices and stories are dispersed throughout *The Everyday Leader.* Sixty-seven people were gracious enough to respond to my queries. While not intended as a broad-scale study, distilling their responses helped clarify and align themes I've heard from clients and through research.

Finally, I labored over the book as my contribution to supporting individuals in realizing the best in themselves and others while getting work done that improves lives and society.

Leaders achieve desired results <u>long-term</u> when they recognize and develop the potential of those entrusted to them.

My Leadership Learning Path

Since my early 20s, I've been fascinated with the stories people have disclosed to me. I leaned into those that revealed the varied paths individuals took to become the person I was experiencing in the present moment. My intrigue with these narratives that shaped and transformed the thinking of all kinds of individuals is likely one reason my husband says... "People love to tell you their stuff." And, mostly, I've been genuinely interested.

It was during my early 20s that my leadership assignments began. I launched into leading with little prior training in what it meant to lead others. I was chosen to lead and mostly relied on people's confidence in me, my goal-oriented nature, and my desire to do something that mattered in the world. We'd get to the goal for sure, though often not with everyone's confidence and a feeling of competence intact.

That first major leadership role, which lasted 20 years, allowed me to succeed, fail, grow...repeat. The work as a young church outreach leader fueled my desire to spend my energies making a difference in society. Fortunately, those with greater authority than I had, immersed me and other young trainees in study around human development and group dynamics as prerequisites for putting us fully in charge.

One of my first and enduring awakenings that shifted the way I looked at people-leadership happened when a member of the church group I was leading said: "Lindiwe, the problem with you working with our group is that you act like everybody is you; everybody is not you. You do some things very well, and seemingly without effort, but they are not natural or that easy for others." At first I received this as a compliment, then understood there was a deeper truth being communicated.

That truth has impacted me ever since; I'm thankful I received this feedback early on my leadership journey. What I was asking of others was what I asked of myself, meaning others' talents and unique ways of seeing the world were mostly un-engaged because I was looking for *my model* of what should be. This new awareness freed me to proceed making effort to shift my approach by concentrating on the distinctive qualities each person possesses and how to put them to good use.

I spent the subsequent two decades of work between independent consulting and nonprofit executive leadership. For a time, I relished the work as an independent consultant because I did not have to supervise anybody! I could work at my own pace and with my own standards of quality without prodding anyone to get with *my program*. I could select subcontractors, let them go after a project closed, or re-engage them if they were a great *fit* for me.

Another of my pivotal junctures was when, as a nonprofit leader, I recognized my need to learn to both hire *and* develop people to execute complex work. In other words, I discovered *my individual greatness* was not enough and could lead to only small-scale difference-making.

Secondly, I learned, after hiring wrong and firing wrong, to slow down and think more deeply about: *What does it mean to lead an effective team, department or organization? What is different about leading oneself and leading others? What could I learn from other perspectives and ways of working? How do I bring inexperienced or less experienced people to realize more of their potential? How long should it take for someone to perform well?*

This inflection point redirected much of my efforts towards developing and inspiring *more* people to increase competence and confidence. This guiding belief emerged for me: *The best use of my resources and talents is to help build other leaders* who in turn can lead others to make a positive, meaningful difference with those they impact at work.

Two Generations of People Work

At the close of 2018, my daughter Noni had finished her first decade of work following undergraduate and MBA degrees in HR talent management. During these years, she grew increasingly interested in management practices, employee engagement and relations, performance management and staff satisfaction. Conversations with her, particularly as a next generation professional, further fueled my inclination to direct my efforts almost exclusively to *people leadership* work.

Upon completion of her undergraduate studies, she was accepted into a large retailer's executive development program. The onboarding and leadership learning process concentrated more on the *business of the business* without much practice on the *business of motivating, leading, developing and evaluating people.* She learned about the company's values, strategy, financial targets and staff performance expectations, but not much about *how to* evoke performance. Following a short shadowing period, she was, at age 22, made the manager for 22 people, all but one much older than her. Like others, she was learning to lead based mostly on trial and error, not specific skill-building in the realm of *people-leadership.*

Her experience as both a middle manager and a supervisee has been a case study of sorts, with periods of success and satisfaction, and times fraught with frustration and challenge. At the time of this writing, she has now reported to five managers over 12 years, two vastly different but good (though later, she reclassified one as not so good because she was nice but expected little and offered little to develop her team members); three she saw as between indifferent to dreadful. This 40% of good or tolerable supervisors is not uncommon.

One of these latter three managers' style was partially responsible for my daughter experiencing a short term, health challenge. Fortunately, she had the financial and emotional support to allow her to leave that job. As a result of this defining moment, she became more selective about *where* she would work and *who* she'd be reporting to.

During her unplanned work sabbatical, she and I had an amazing experience as work partners, spending a year developing a coaching and consulting business. Supporting the growth of *everyday leaders* became our shared pursuit.

The Everyday Leader: WHAT

This book offers thoughts and actionable steps for becoming highly effective leading people. That's it. When I say effective, I am referring to creating and sustaining an environment in which those being led by you are both highly productive and quite pleased to be working with you and the organization.

What it isn't. This book is not *directly* about business systems, best practices in finance, strategy or marketing, or leading quantum change. The book, however, supports experts in such areas who have people reporting to them. As 21st Century leaders are aware, achieving exceptional business performance consistently requires skills to grow and inspire the people in our charge. The *human aspect* of work often makes or breaks the leader and the organization.

The Everyday Leader: WHO

Every day we come across leaders at various levels that impact us in small or large ways. You are likely one of them. Think of the store manager, chief executive, board chair, the school department head, supervisor, committee chairs, the local small business owner, parent association president, etc.

Interactions with everyday leaders, some who may only momentarily be in charge of us, can change our mood, affect our health, make our day better or worse, even change the trajectory of our careers.

Reading this book will benefit anyone who has responsibility to motivate, develop, manage, and lead people to get stuff done. Supervisors, chiefs of all kinds, entrepreneurs, directors, managers, chairpersons, parent group leaders, virtual team leaders, and more will find something to tweak your *people leader* skills.

Everyday Leader: HOW it's structured

The book is organized to support you in getting to the *people* actions and strategies that best fit you and your goals as they change over time. There are three sections, organized around Know and Grow themes, described below.

Part One: Know Today's Work Environment for Leading Others. This section offers contextual information about leading people in contemporary times while building the case for continuous learning for leaders at every level. It examines what the experts have to say about the success factors, challenges and impacts that tie directly to the leader's efficacy in maximizing the talents of those entrusted to them. This section also takes a look at some contemporary competency requirements for leading in an ever-changing environment, knowing that job titles will only take us so far.

There are summaries of concepts and models for leaders to either use as is or adapt to provide an optimal environment for their and their team's success.

Part Two: Know and Grow Yourself. This section is 100% focused on YOU. These five chapters cover such matters as building high-level self-awareness; clarifying what your role needs from you; inventorying your existing and underused inner resources; pinpointing the beliefs, strengths and opportunities that foster or limit your effectiveness; using the *power* and weight of your role wisely; designing your growth plan; developing a synergistic team; and designing a healthy, high-achievement work culture.

The section begins with a special chapter titled: *The Leadership Launch.* If you are beginning a new leadership role, whether it's a first ever leader role or transitioning to a new executive role that requires you to supervise others, you want to start here. Positioning yourself well with people and within the organization or team starting before your first day makes all the difference to what happens during the ensuing few years. Enough said... find chapter 5.

Part Three: Know and Grow Your People. The five chapters in this section address specific areas and strategies for masterfully leading and growing your direct reports. It's framed around the Five Keys to Leading Others. Those keys are *Lead & Align, Connect, Coach, Develop and Perform.* A portion of Chapter 10 addresses communication competence, a soft, powerful skillset that enables the leader's success across all Five Keys.

Practical tools: Throughout the book, you will see attention has been paid to practical application, things you can think about and actually try out. There are clear, simple charts and tables, worksheets, reflections, checklists, and more that help readers grasp and apply specific ideas quickly. The Appendix includes five extra worksheets to support your work.

Anticipate the book being one that you reach for repeatedly on your journey—for a process or a reminder.

Suggestion

Read a chapter weekly, find at least one nugget to put to use as you lead your people to their best work.

Thanks for taking this journey and allowing me to share mine with you. Let's dig in!

Part One

Know the Work Environment for Leading Others

"People do not wake up in the morning and think to themselves, 'I want to go to work and fail miserably today, do a terrible job, make everyone's life around me awful, and I want to come home and feel really bad about myself at the end of the day.[1]'"

[1] Bichelmeyer, B. A., *Performance Improvement Quarterly*, 12:4, 1999, p. 84

This statement stuck with me since I read it years ago. It helped reframe my approach to leading the few individual direct reports that I found challenging. I believe that 95% of the time, the statement is accurate: *People don't come to work to make you, them and everyone else miserable.*

Those in the workplace performance field often cite this quote as they work to uncover *why* people are succeeding or failing at work. For many of those dreary or dispassionate employees, they arrive day after day to find no magic wand has magically transformed their workplace into a supportive and inspiring experience, helmed by a competent people-leader.

Part One looks at the larger work setting in which you will lead. Explore it early in your leadership assignment. Seasoned leaders may need to address the changing leadership trends, as well, and their implications for how you to shift your practices today. This section is the foundation for Parts Two and Three.

This section has four chapters:

1. Facing the Leadership Facts

2. Common Leadership Ascension Patterns

3. Leading in the 21st Century, Different from Yesteryears

4. The High-performance Work Environment

What is true is already so. Owning up to it doesn't make it worse. Not being open about it doesn't make it go away. [2]

Chapter 01
Facing the Leadership Facts

Coming to terms with the nature of leadership today, along with acknowledging a leader's strengths and challenges can offer insights and reveal possibilities that had not been considered. *Owning up doesn't make it worse.* Those desiring to capably lead people can benefit from the perspectives in this chapter. They may prompt you to fine-tune your practices as you pursue better work results and greater fulfillment.

The chapter's topics are: 1) common facts and data on leaders' success, failure and impact at work, and 2) a snapshot of 67 interviewees' input on leader practices.

---

[2] Eugene T. Gendlin, *Focusing*, 1978

1. Common facts and data points

I have borrowed the most salient *facts* from prominent leadership polling and research organizations to paint a picture for you. You'll see findings from Gallup, Center for Creative Leadership, Harvard Business Review, and others represented in the table that begins below.

Sharing these nuggets is meant to encourage not discourage you. These 10 summarize the complexity and effect of leader practices on their people. These set the table for why and how *The Everyday Leader* can invigorate your commitment to build proficiency as you lead others. Use the *facts* to inform and build awareness sufficient to prompt you to take action to refine your way forward. Jim Collins' classic words from *Good to Great* are reminders:

"You absolutely cannot make a series of good decisions without first confronting the brutal facts."

10 facts paint a picture...

1.	A full 60% of first-time managers receive no training for how to be a manager. (CCL)[3]
2.	Up to 40% of new leaders derail in the first 18 months. (multiple sources)
3.	55% of leaders have poor interpersonal relationships and 47% have an unwillingness or inability to change or adapt. (CCL- ccl.org)

[3] *Develop Leaders, Not Just Bosses*, ccl.org, Feb. 1, 2021

4. A mere 21% of employees feel they are supervised in a way to motivate outstanding performance. (Gallup State of American Workplace, 2017)
5. Only 11% of direct reports would go to their supervisor for advice.[4]
6. 70% of direct reports say their supervisor is the most stressful part of their day, and 70% say their supervisor is either unprepared or ineffective. (Gallup and American Psychological Association)
7. 65% of employees say they prefer a new boss over a raise.[5]
8. Organizations fail to choose the candidate with the right talent for the manager job a whopping 82% of the time.[6]
9. 54% of leaders acknowledge they don't have all the skills they need to do their jobs.[7]
10. 50% of employees cite their boss as the reason for quitting their jobs. (Gallup, SOAW 2017)

So, there's high probability that employees will work for an incompetent leader during their careers. Your growth will grow the ranks of competent leaders.

I've shared data points like these with leaders and teams, and some found them enlightening with directional clues, others were incredulous and disheartened. The latter I assume is because it feels personal, making it difficult not to react to facts and evidence that infer we as leaders need to do better. And we can. As you reflect on this list of facts, know that you can take specific, attainable actions to grow and tap into your reservoir of expansive capabilities.

[4] Zenger and Stinnett. *Extraordinary Coach*, 2010, p. 59
[5] Anderson, A. R., How a bad boss can make you sick, *Forbes Magazine*, 10/28/ 2014
[6] *State of the American Manager*, Gallup, 2015, p. 7
[7] Bessen, J. Workers don't have the skills they need and they know it 9/17/2014, HBR

2. Interviewee's input on leader practices (2021)

Having worked with leaders at various levels and career stages, I wanted to hear their voices around what *people leadership* looked and felt like for them. I gathered input from 67 people during 2021. I've also referenced several clients' stories to be sure to hear from a diverse cross-section about *people leader* practices. The stories throughout *The Everyday Leader* are from those aged 28-71, representing diverse racial, age, and gender identities.

Below I've summarized the 67 interviewees' input from two perspectives: *leading others* and from the vantage point of *being led* (as direct reports). Take a look at their thoughts and highlight those items where you concur and importantly, areas that you hadn't given attention but are worth bearing in mind.

Themes from the leader's (supervisor's) perspective

Question: What are the attributes and behaviors of the BEST people-leaders? They....

- Cast and share a vision, give people something to live up to.
- Develop others; believe in the capacity of their people.
- Have passion for the work.
- Possess strong critical thinking skills.
- Surround themselves with talented people without insecurity.
- Are culturally competent.
- Remove roadblocks for their teams.
- Set goals and ensure accountability in partnership with each of their direct reports.

- Are ongoing learners, intentional about getting better.
- Are good listeners, open to alternative ways of getting things done.
- Know how to have *fierce* conversations with empathy and respect.
- Provide clear tasks, expectations, tools and support to do the job.
- Effectively delegate.
- Seek feedback from direct reports.
- Praise and recognize freely.
- Spend time learning the styles, strengths and challenges of each direct report.

Question: What are the attributes and behaviors of the LEAST SKILLED people-leaders? They...

- Micro/over-manage staff and are authoritative.
- Give unclear directions, causing staff to do the wrong work or re-work.
- Are poor at prioritizing.
- Abuse their power with direct reports.
- Avoid addressing the problems, allowing matters to get worse.
- Act like only "my way" works; threatened by diverse thinking.
- Blame others for their lack of success.
- Distrust their staff; overly watchful.
- Don't include team in planning the work.
- Use intimidation to get work done.
- Don't learn from mistakes.
- Take a cookie cutter approach to managing every person.
- Take credit for others' work.
- Are poor listeners.

It's useful to balance leaders' views with their direct reports' thoughts about the leaders' perceptions of their effectiveness. Research is consistent in pointing out a perception divide between how well leaders and employees believe the leaders are performing related to leading those on their teams.

From the direct reports' perspective

The following input, from the perspective of being a direct report, is similar though with greater emphasis on how the leader treats people.

Question: What are the attributes and behaviors of the BEST supervising managers? They....

- Are genuine, humane, respectful and interested in all staff.
- Let people know their job position is important and valued.
- Inspire the team around a vision.
- Acknowledge talents and motivations of each staffer.
- Are proactive in creating an empowering culture.
- Have high expectations and hold self and team accountable.
- Encourage autonomy and self-direction, while providing support .
- Provide compassionate, corrective feedback and support.
- Advocate for their staff members.
- Ensure the tools and resources needed to do a good job are provided.
- Practice transparency, so people know what's going on.
- Are open to diverse people, thoughts and ideas.
- Act as brainstorming and thinking partner.
- Follow through on promises.
- Are informed, knowledgeable, and resourceful.
- Model a good work ethic.
- Focus on organization AND the staff.
- Create opportunities for staff to develop/grow.
- Act as a mentor, not just a boss.

Question: What are the attributes and behaviors of the least skilled people-leaders (supervisors)? They...

- Are scattered without a clear vision, reactive.
- Don't value direct reports *off work* time.
- Do little self-reflection; blindness to poor, antiquated, manager style.
- Are uninformed and unprepared.
- Lack empathy and interest in direct reports.
- Don't delegate; try to do it all.
- Are not easily accessible; closed door policy.
- Are authoritative, overbearing.
- Only get input from a select few, causing bad, biased decisions.
- Assume the worst in people.
- Are closed to new ways of doing things.
- Prone to open displays of favoritism.
- Have horrible people skills; speak "down" to the staff; disrespectful, raising voice, commanding tone, bullying, overly critical.
- Are indecisive.
- Hold poorly planned, time-wasting meetings.
- Are self-promoting, self-serving, taking all the credit- "no space for anyone else to grow."
- Create an "every person for themselves" environment.

What one thing stuck out most for you as you reviewed the responses from leaders and direct reports?

____

____

Finally, I asked the interviewees to share tips they'd offer anyone leading a group of people. As you review these top 10 tips, summarized from the 67 respondents' input, identify any you might want to look at more closely.

Top 10 tips for leading direct reports

1. Be aware that being a great leader doesn't just happen; it takes intentional work and practice.
2. Trust that most employees want to do a good job each day.
3. Manage people with care, respect and empathy balanced with clarity, support and accountability.
4. Really listen and understand the views and feelings of others.
5. Seek, hear and respect staff opinions.
6. Passionately and clearly articulate vision, beliefs and goals; then inspire and clarify expectations.
7. Know that the culture you set up will determine the success of the team you lead.
8. Discover and utilize each direct report's strengths to the fullest to advance the work and their sense of worth.
9. Prioritize time to coach, develop and support direct reports.
10. Acknowledge people (*Hello, Thank you*, etc.), celebrate job successes regularly, and make room for fun.

Activity: Based on the 10 Tips, fill in responses to these two statements:

1.Two of my areas of great strength are item #s _____ _____

2. One main area for additional development is item#: _____

Some of the interviewees' specific stories are included in *The Everyday Leader* in relevant chapters. What is undeniable is that their actual experiences, along with large study conclusions, support the idea that there is a small set of drivers of work satisfaction, engagement and performance. Daniel Pink identified three in his popular book, *Drive, What Motivates People at Work.* He contends that the secrets to getting the best from people boil down to *1)* ***autonomy*** *(a chance to carry out my efforts with empowerment and self-direction), 2)* ***mastery*** *(chances to create and learn), and 3)* ***purpose*** *(feeling what I do is making a positive difference).* Other studies include another powerful motivator, ***relatedness*** (feeling connected to others).

This wraps up *Chapter 1, Facing the Leadership Facts.* As you move through the chapters, remember it's one thing to name what's needed to be effective, but to know what to do and how to do it is quite another. Human patterns are stubborn and repetitive, yours and mine included. So, keep reading.

All of the subsequent chapters offer you tips and strategies to embed key performance motivators into the workplace and enhance the achievement and satisfaction of those you lead.

It takes considerable courage to answer your inner voice when it says, "I don't know what I'm doing!" by seeking help to grow as a leader.[8]

Chapter 02

Common Leadership Ascension Patterns

Taking stock of the typical ways people move into leadership roles can be both instructive and humbling. The varied ascension patterns partly explains the disparities in the quality of the employee experience today. The aim is that this chapter prompts enough humility to inspire leaders to work on their readiness to lead others. If so, you are joining a communal but unspoken sense that "I don't know what I'm doing." That's OK, because you can shift your mindset and begin directing energy towards preparing to lead others skillfully.

This second chapter highlights 1) Leadership ascension patterns, 2) constructing a leadership viewpoint, and 3) derailment—common, costly and correctable. There is a correlation between these three sets of information.

[8] Evje, B. Are you worthy of leadership? *Forbes Magazine*, 6/23/2021.

1. Leadership ascension patterns

How did you rise to your current leadership assignment? What factors converged to bestow upon you the honor of leading and managing others? These questions are not meant to deflate the joy of landing a leadership job, nor question your ability to do it. There are common patterns related to how a person elevates up the leader ladder, which have implications for how they should prepare to succeed in that role. I've underscored six here; I'm sure there are others.

Six common patterns: A considerable number of today's leaders have been *Thrust into Leadership*, that is, they became what's referred to as *Accidental Leaders*. That type of new leader traveled through one or a combination of the first five pathways identified here:

1) selected based on their *potential* to do the job (e.g., interest, commitment, and education)

2) the leader performed well as an individual contributor (excellent in a prior subject matter expert role that didn't include leading others)

3) as a reward for time served in a previous job, *warranting* upward movement as a retention strategy

4) the new leader had the right connections and was championed by someone with enough influence to get them the

job (e.g., inheriting a family business or benefitting from the *friend network.*)

5) no one else wanted to lead, often the case in volunteer roles or roles that are hard to fill (so a less-preferred candidate wins the job)

6) intentionally prepared to lead others at a higher level

Those in category 6 might have arrived at their roles 1) as a result of a succession planning process (not just succession identification); 2) by using a targeted development plan; 3) engaged in structured mentoring, coaching or shadowing initiatives; 5) worked with the hiring supervisor to develop a comprehensive onboarding, culture integration and transition plan; or 5) took the initiative to conduct self-study, etc.

Neither of the first five patterns is inherently good or bad; they are just that—patterns that might indicate the need for the perceptive new hire to plan how to be successful, rather than just jump in and do what they've always done.

A case that backfired: I worked with a client who was accustomed to "getting stuff done." He demanded his new staff (including yelling) produce his version of excellence in his first-time CEO role. He quickly fired those who didn't "get it done" or who pushed back against his intimidating style. He reminded one staffer, "I'm the boss now, and it won't be like it used to be." The leader was clueless about the organization's culture, community stature or the network of key stakeholders, including the board. In under a year, after relocating his family and buying a home, he was terminated. The board had initially appreciated his "get stuff done" drive but not at the expense of the staff or their stature in the small community.

He arrived in the role based on past success somewhere else, without recognizing some of his past practices didn't land well in a new situation. His ascendancy appeared to be tied to a combination of numbers 1, 3, 4 and 5 from the list.

The hiring of this leader wasn't a bad choice necessarily. He and the board, however, made assumptions that could have been addressed if more of number 6 had been tackled.

Reflection: Consider the six ascension patterns.

1. Which do you believe best reflects how you arrived at your current role? It may be a combination of factors. ________
2. What do you wish you had known or done that would have made taking the new role even more successful?______

   ____

   ____

   ____

What's widely recognized is: Despite the way a leader comes into their role, most are not provided critical job transition support. When hastily assigned or elevated into roles that require them to lead others, the leader (and the organization's) inattention to effective transition planning can result in unfortunate outcomes. *Chapter 5: Considerations for Your Launch into Leadership* offers actionable insights to mitigate this challenge to free the leader to move forward successfully.

2. **Constructing a leadership viewpoint**

How did you learn what to do or think as a leader? What model of leadership are you using? Is it a clear and deliberate approach or are you content to just see what happens?

Leaders who have never been exposed to good developmental leaders tend to mimic what they've seen in their experience being supervised. They tend to adopt the habits of their ill-equipped leader as a prototype for leading others. And their previous leader likely borrowed their practices from their experience too. So, a continuous cycle of poor practices ensues, one that harms those with little choice on who supervises them.

A client while considering how to better communicate with her team, shared: *"I realize based on what you're having me think about, I've NEVER reported to a good leader. I've done to others what was done to me. I've been a boss, sometimes I throw my authority around, and I've acted like I know more than I actually do. I reflected an aggressiveness that likely came from insecurity of not knowing what I'm doing."*

The story reveals a breakthrough awareness that enabled this brilliant school leader to round out her competencies to get the most out of her team by learning to listen, ask questions, coach, provide meaningful feedback, and more confidently delegate tasks. These actions, based on her staff's feedback, increased their motivation, their belief that she had their backs, grew their skills, expanded the scope of their work and freed this leader to work at a more strategic level. She stopped bossing and began using a more masterful leader style.

Do any of these sound like how you came to form your leadership approach/philosophy?

- ✓ I just did the best I could, relying on common sense.
- ✓ I mostly modeled supervising others from my own experience with leaders to whom I reported.
- ✓ I did what I've always done that worked in the past, and I assumed it would continue to work.
- ✓ I engaged in study and practice of contemporary people management practices.
- ✓ I participated in coaching, mentoring or shadowing to prepare me for my new role.
- ✓ I was part of a succession planning process that helped build the skills I needed to lead others at the next level.

- ✓ I went through a great onboarding process that helped close the gaps between skills I possessed and the skills required for the job.

Make a note: What did you or others do that helped you get ready to be effective in your role?

____

____

____

The conundrum of mimicking your experience: In the best cases, copying how you've been supervised offers some lessons; in the worst cases, your learning is hard won, fraught with anguish. In settings when you've seen good leaders in action, you've gathered some tips. Even so, at some point you discover that trying to replicate what Gallup's 10% of star managers do falls short in equipping you to competently lead others.

Being in close proximity to good leadership practices doesn't necessarily ready you for the role. Having role models is great, just not enough.

The practices and style of one leader don't always play well with another, and their contexts for leading may differ, thus calling for different approaches. There are specific skills required to lead others, and a leader's philosophical foundation and individual style (from which their practices take shape) are also factors. Unless you embrace those same beliefs about work and people, you are likely to be seen as inauthentic or mimicking others. *Chapters 6 and 7* can support you in identifying your *people* beliefs, authentic style and unique strengths.

Modeling a past leader. I asked an acquaintance (a new manager) to identify great manager characteristics. She shared something like this: *"I learned to be a manager after working for a manager I disliked. Later, when I became a supervising manager, I realized she was really good – pushy, deadline driven, uncompromising. We got the work done with her, even though she was impersonal, micromanaging, and insensitive to my family needs. I lead my team the same way because the bottom line is, we have to get stuff done."*

She is likely unknowingly terrorizing her new team just as she had been. She's imitating ineffective practices, while getting deeply entrenched into a belief system that infers: *You have to be tough on people at work for them to produce.*

3. Derailment—Common, costly, correctable

Wow, she's really good with people. Somehow, she gets people motivated to get tons of work finished and even go the extra mile.

When I heard this statement, I thought it portrays someone possessing a leadership skill considered one of the keys to success at all levels. According to studies, **the ability (or**

inability) to mold and lead a staff team is among the top factors in leadership success or derailment.

Derailment means *falling off the tracks,* a train analogy used in the leadership field. It's when leaders, believed to be high potentials, suddenly and surprisingly self-destruct—evident in stalled careers, demotions or terminations. Becoming familiar with the typical causes reveals derailment is predictable and reversible; and the onus is on both the leader and their manager to prevent a descent. Between months six and 18, it becomes apparent that a derailing leader is on a path to failure.

Good news: Derailment is avoidable and correctable despite data showing 40 to 50% of leaders derail on their new jobs within the first 18 months.

That 40 to 50% doesn't consider the numbers of leaders who are flawed but remain in their roles. They have a lot of time to cause interminable suffering for those in their charge.

The most common and costly derailment factors: Know that your success is critical across stakeholder groups, so recognize, in most cases, no one starts out wanting you to fail. Adopt the mindset that "they want me to succeed." It's not so much that they love you deeply before you even start, it's that the cost of failure has huge ramifications—for the organization, staff and of course for you, the leader. Some adverse effects of losing a new leader are loss productivity for you and your direct reports, consumption of time hiring and preparing interim staff, the ramp up time for onboarding your replacement, and untold dollars lost due to diminished staff morale.

Management organizations have examined what causes high-potential leaders to be ineffective. To a great extent, they came up with the same or combinations of these characteristics:

- *Problems with interpersonal relationships*
- *Difficulty molding and developing staff*
- *Trouble adapting to change, resistance to new ideas*
- *Unwillingness to collaborate*
- *Failure to meet business goals, mediocre performance*
- *Strategic differences with managers or boards*
- *Not learning from mistakes*

The chart below summarizes these major causes. Several are related to failure to lead, engage, inspire, and mobilize *people.*

These issues tend to surface in various ways: *lack of political savvy, poor communication, naivete about the complexity of*

work, staff complaints about your style, poor chemistry and alignment with the managing board, low staff morale, lack of clear direction, incapacity for constructive dissent, lack of inclusion of different perspectives, poor collaboration and teaming skills, undermining colleagues, etc.

Remember, derailment can be avoided or mitigated by taking preemptive steps to prepare yourself to lead. It's advisable for you and your hiring manager to proactively create planned activities to establish the foundation for early and sustained success in your leader role.

Derailment averted. *"I'm a seasoned executive. I've been successful for decades. Everything I touched seemed to turn to gold, except now. Things are changing so fast, demanding something more and different. I'm not sure how I can position myself to succeed. What worked for me in the past is not working."* He's aware that he's headed for derailment without intervention. This client acted by first assessing his *learning*/growth needs, determining what he needed to *unlearn*, and he began to grow and demonstrate effectiveness in his new role. He, the board and staff released sighs of relief.

This leader demonstrated the emotional maturity to honestly face his situation. He possessed or built the psychological stamina to make needed mindset and behavior changes in enough time to change course.

We all have tendencies to relapse into past habits that could reduce the potency of our strengths in a new setting. We also have blind spots (some of which will be new blind spots that arise in a new context). So, think about and respond to this question, then make a "note to self" below.

What qualities or habits should I address early, even if I feel great about my preparedness to lead others or if I've been thrust into leadership?

Note to self: Pay attention to the following factors that may be critical to my success in this leadership role:

____

____

____

This ends *Chapter 2, Common Leadership Ascension Patterns.* As a reminder, this part of the book is designed to set the stage for you to adopt a growth mindset throughout your leadership journey. You want to make the best use of your boundless potential to be successful as a leader. Strategies and suggestions for increased *people mastery* are in Parts 2 and 3.

The workplace is a "human" culture. Your job is to lead in ways that facilitates people actualizing their potential as they pursue achieving meaningful goals.

Chapter 03

Leading in the 21st Century, Different from Yesteryears

Archaic approaches to leading people in business and the nonprofit sector are plentiful and pervasive. They are vestiges from a world long gone and are no longer in step with today's realities. These *old school* leader behaviors are not only problematic for younger workers, called Generations Y and Z. Most people, notwithstanding age, gender, or racial differences would be ecstatic if better leader methods were widespread. The best leaders are growth-oriented; they are relentless about acquiring contemporary leader competence, which requires greater "people" adeptness than 50, even 10, years ago.

Chapter 3 addresses two topics: 1) *Bossing*, a relic of the past, and 2) call to continually sharpen leader competencies.

1. *Bossing*, a relic of the past

Are your leadership methods frozen in time? Despite the proliferation of technology and easy access to all levels of knowledge, management practices have changed very little since Frederick Taylor's (who passed away in 1915) Industrial Age management efficiency theories. Neither the strong-armed bosses nor the title-obsessed bureaucrat will be effective much longer in today's landscape.

> *"Management practices...have not kept pace with what has happened in society. Remarkably little has changed when it comes to the basics of management. If a middle manager in a firm had consumed some magic potion and fallen asleep 50 years ago and suddenly awakened (much like Rip van Winkle), there is a good chance that he could fit right into the management structure today if his company still existed."* [9]

Think about that. The world has undergone seismic shifts over the last 50 years, yet leadership practices have remained relatively stagnant as if *The Earth Stood Still*. Even some of the university programs fail to capture and prepare people for the quantum changes in the world of work.

Regrettably, even younger managers aren't immune to embracing archaic behaviors and lack regard for workers'

[9] Zenger and Stinnett, *The Extraordinary Coach*, p. 48.

humanity. They, too, may bark orders, believing their verbally aggressive approach will prompt high productivity. Many mature workers have resigned or chose early retirement to escape these overachieving boss-leaders and to revitalize their health after years of work-related stress. That's why a college degree is rarely enough to equip you to be the best leader today.

Imagine, for example, an incarcerated person, after a 30-year sentence, who finally gets exonerated and released. The things they took for granted in the life left behind have vanished or changed so radically they're unrecognizable. They have to get acclimated to smartphones, social media, streaming video, online bill pay, online shopping and more.

This same person, happy to get a job to restore self-sufficiency, is likely startled, however, to find how easy it is to fit right back in at work. The manager is just like the ones 30 years ago--bossing, controlling, checking timecards closely, inflexible and with eyes peering over their shoulder—just like before.

Bossing is from a time when most non-managerial workers were trained to be dutiful, sweaty order-takers. Today (the 21st Century), bossing, with its outmoded, punishing paradigm, is limited. The power of prodding, bullying, and demanding workers to produce is waning. More workers are resisting it (overtly demanding better treatment or by moving on as fast as they can).

"Bossing" is not to be confused with assertive, decisive, and results-oriented leadership. Bossing is oppressive, dominating, and arrogant, while leading, coaching and collaborating resonate better with staff and evoke higher performance.

Today's workers are adept at finding their own answers and contributing their ideas to organizations. They yearn for autonomy, agency to make decisions appropriate to their roles, collaboration (with a range of communities), flatter structures (that value input from all levels of the organization), and opportunities to engage their brains creatively. They want clarity on the organization's vision and direction and how their own values align.

It's imperative that leaders figure out how to lead people TODAY. With unending access to information, people don't come to work as empty vessels.

High talent workers are less likely to commit to a job simply for the money. They have confidence in their skills and will offer them without reservation when the leader and the workplace enable, foster, and value creatively integrating their talents.

What evolution is needed to extricate yourself from outmoded industrial age practices and embrace approaches better aligned with a knowledge-rich, people-centered environment?

Comparison of changing times at work

50 Years Ago	Today
Top-down strategy and decision making	Shared leadership, influencing style, trust, engagement from bottom up, participatory
Bossing (Top down, rigid hierarchical standards)	Developing, inspiring, empowering, collaborative, flatter egalitarian culture
Selective or withholding information	Encourages accessing information 24/7
Command and control	Allows for risk, failure and innovation
Rewards rule-following	Rewards creativity, problem solving and performance
Motivates via strictly monetary incentives	Includes rewarding with purpose, greater freedom, and opportunities for mastery
Views people as expenses	Recognizes people as assets with strengths to leverage
Rigid reliance on best practices (based on *past* proven strategies)	Engages both best and breakthrough practices (more future focused and innovative)

Think about it: Where do you stand?

1. Are your leadership approaches more consistent with the left or right side of the table ? Left_____ Right _____

2. Do you think of people more as expenses *or* assets and resources to achieve the goals? Expenses____ Assets ____

It's not just Millennials: Classified as those born approximately between 1980 and 1995, Millennials are seen as tech-savvy and needing flexibility, freedom, voice, and balance (work is not *life* itself"). Their generation bears the brunt of criticism and stereotypes about being difficult to manage (especially by older workers). They are labeled as disloyal (to their companies), demanding, self-absorbed and slackers.

It's a fallacy. Other generations, maybe less vocal, would be delighted to have many of these same human-valuing experiences and opportunities as those many Millennials insist on. Most of the 67 responding to my questionnaire about the best and worst manager practices, despite their age (28-71), gender, and race, showed remarkable consistency in their suggestions to managers—get to know, value, engage, listen to, and grow those who report to them.

Think Again: The similarities common across all generations doesn't preclude the fact that there are some distinctive differences in work preferences and habits based on age-related norms. Be aware that there may be four generations occupying the same workspace, and leaders need to become masterful with all of them. Questions for you:

1. In your workplace, do you find yourself challenged by any particular worker age group? Y__ N__ If so, which one? ____________________________________

2. Identify just one way you can improve how you engage with them by understanding their and your particular patterns, considering the information about changing workplace characteristics on pages 42 and 43. I can ____.

Movements demand more from the workplace. With the advocacy from women's rights, Civil Rights, racial justice, and other identity Movements, the expectation and insistence on equal pay, voice, and respect have contributed to the demand for a more humane and equitable workplace. Several social changes have converged to offer workers broad exposure to new ways of thinking and acting. As a result, people are "smarter" than decades ago; they can discern incompetence and insecurity more quickly in an environment ruled by the antiquated hierarchical structuralists. They are less afraid to voice their views or leave the organization.

It's best, then, to assume ALL workers want to be treated as people—valued, cared about, engaged, growing, respected and seen as contributors. Portraying one generation or those celebrating their diverse identities as *difficult* won't address the real issues related to competence to lead others well.

After more than 100 years of controlling and cajoling people into outstanding performance, the death knell has rung:

Old-style leaders who prime people to be compliant, fearful, and conforming to their controls of time,

resources, and work structures are conditioning workers to be of limited help to organizations that need to innovate in today's dynamic environment.

The acquiescent workers, whipped into shape by boss-leaders, quietly bide their time. They merely do their jobs and have low engagement and investment in the success of an organization.

2. Keep sharpening your skills

For continuing relevance and value in your role, embrace a growth mindset and stay on a course to increase your leader competence. Leader traits for today's economy are not static.

People skills as important as technical ones. The work of leading to high accomplishment is *people-oriented.* Leaders today focus on people, their capabilities and their potential.

> *People are part of the core energy of organizations. Equipment and financial reserves are important, but people are the heart and soul of organizations...People are behind everything that happens.*" [10]

The ability to engage and leverage people's talents is an indisputable requirement. We now witness leaders entering roles in business areas with little technical experience; they can hire direct reports who have that industry-specific expertise.

---

[10] Van Tiem, D., Moseley, J., and Dessinger, J., *Fundamentals of Performance Improvement*, 2012, p. 7

What these leaders bring and deploy is the capacity to envision the future and inspire people to collectively bring it to fruition.

Today's *people leader* avoids micromanaging, and instead *directs much of their energies to creating the optimum conditions* for people to do their best work with profound passion. These masterful leaders focus on *directing the team members' energies towards problem solving, increased effectiveness and goal achievement.*

A general leader competency model

Many leaders in new roles establish a habit of "faking it" with the hope they finally "make it." Astute observers (often direct reports) see through this *pretending.* The accidental leader's behavioral blunders are telltale signs of their "faking it."

An alternative to "faking it" (and the insecurities that come with that) is to assess the variance between the talents that landed you the job and the capabilities needed for the new role. The middle circle below, once clarified, defines the targets for your development plan. (See Chapter 5 for a suggested plan.)

Reviewing general or the organization's leadership competency models can also be instructive. There are many models to be found on the Internet. Below, I share one developed by a group of middle managers with whom I worked. I thought it would be empowering for them to think through what a 21st Century leadership model looked like, without looking at other "proven" ones. These *Everyday Leaders* divided their model into two sets of skills and attributes (Task-Centric and People-Centric).

TRY THIS: Review their leadership competency model and place a checkmark (✓) by competencies where you are very strong, circle (O) the ones that are growth areas, and if unsure, (U).

Task-Centric "Getting Exceptional Work Done"	People Centric "Creating a Staff Culture for Success"
• Visionary & Strategic • Decisive • Good Business Acumen • Role-specific Skills & Competencies • Professionalism • Collaborative • Influencing • Accountable/Reliable • Risk taking/ Innovative • Committed to Mission • Change adaptable • Diplomatic	• Emotionally Mature • Empathetic/Humane • Honest and Trusting • Connects/Friendly • Effective, clear communicator • Good Listener/Patient • Inspiring/ Motivating (Fun) • Effective Feedback • People Developer • Transparent • Being "present" with people

Depending on your specific role, there may be other critical competencies that take precedence over some of those selected for this group's model. Think through what those might be.

Additional competencies important for success in my role:
____

____

This closes *Chapter 3, Leading in the 21st Century*. It addressed contemporary trends related to leading people. This may help you "fine-tune or align your leadership skills and style to better predict your success.

Strive to create a workplace where people are always respected, valued, inspired, challenged, and empowered, and they will exceed expectations.

Chapter 04
The High-Performance Work Environment

Increasingly, in today's workplace, people want leaders to have the wherewithal to establish an environment that makes work meaningful, empowering and productive. So, try to spend most of your time figuring out how to put in place and sustain a people-oriented, people-supportive work environment that compels the team's best accomplishments.

Chapter 4 addresses one of the most important aspects of your work as a leader. It reminds you of the power and responsibility you have to either propel your direct reports towards high *or* low-quality performance. The chapter topics: 1) Features of a quality performance environment, and 2) fine-tune the work environment to maximize outcomes.

1. Features of a quality performance environment

How would it strike you if a workplace performance expert said: *"80 to 85% of the extent to which people achieve at work has more to do with factors in the work environment rather than the individual"?*

Since the leader is largely responsible for the quality of the work environment, that might feel pretty weighty. Some leaders were taken aback or balked at the idea when I shared this anecdotal nugget from the field of human performance. *"There's no way you will ever convince me of that!" "You're saying I as the leader am 80% of the reason people do their jobs." "This sounds so individually disempowering."*

This 80-85% guesstimate related to the impact the quality of the work context has on how well people do their jobs doesn't mean any of these things. In reality, embracing this data point empowers YOU as a leader. Keep reading.

The graphic that follows summarizes the most common work environment factors that affect how well people perform and engage at work. You can use it to enhance your staff members' fulfillment and work accomplishments. Pay attention to the middle and right boxes. These elements are the performance influencers that matter most and those over which you have the greatest control.

Model of Work Performance Factors

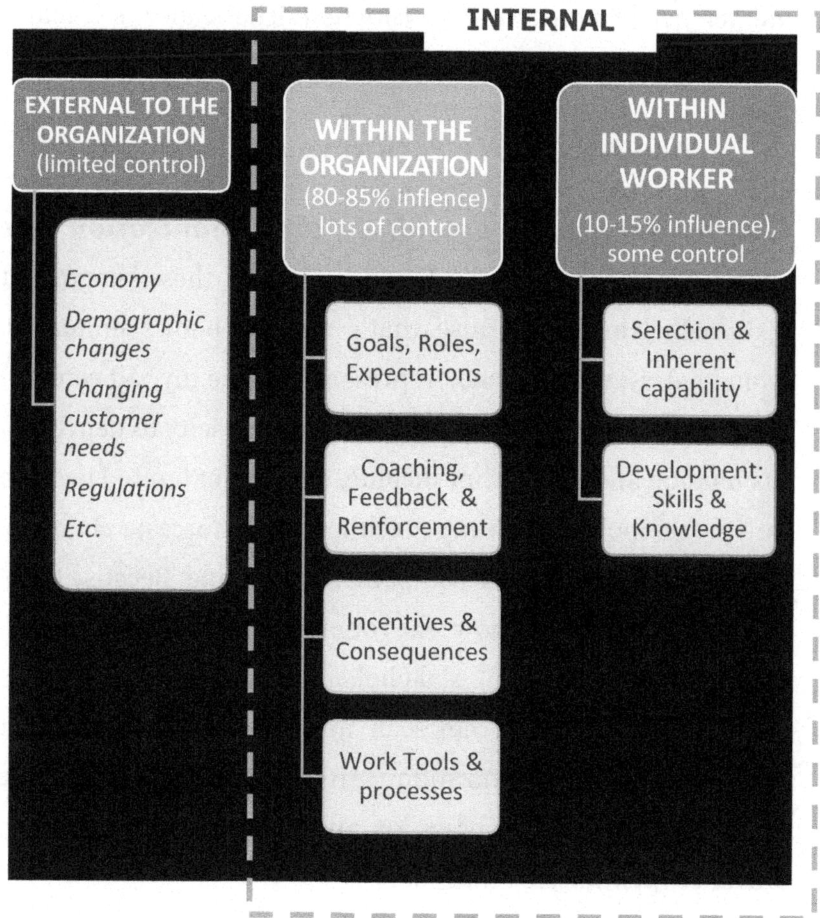

The illustration shows that there are six major "Internal" factors that interact with each other to explain why some people perform well and others don't: *Goals and Roles, Coaching and Reinforcing Feedback, Incentives and Consequences, Tools and Processes, and Selection and Development.* These are areas to assess and observe their quality and then refine them as you *endeavor to lead people to higher performance and satisfaction.* The leader is a major force related to the "Within the Organization" items' quality.

About the Three Performance Categories

Things happening outside of the organization. *The Everyday Leader* book doesn't address these important external elements because that's not the book's emphasis. Nonetheless, what this box represents are the myriad external influences that impact an organization's capacity to deliver on its mission and goals. They include, but are not limited to, such areas as political, legal, technological forces; changing customer needs; and the competitive landscape. Because these dynamics can alter how the organization moves forward, leaders engage their stakeholders in organization-wide strategy, during which they scan for external trends and their impact on the organization. After that, they determine strategies to either leverage or mitigate those influences to advance their mission and goals.

Things happening internal to the organization. All or most of these factors are within YOUR sphere of control—at least to some degree. And even if you're not at the top, you can work on most of these within your specific area of work.

I've done enough work with organizations and leaders to conclude that as common as these seem, many elements are not in place or just marginally. For example, lots of workers don't know what their organizations' goals are or how their work links to them. So, they are satisfied to do just "get my job done." Imagine the difference if they were reminded and inspired by how their jobs tie directly to some great purpose.

Leaders can misinterpret why some staff members descend into low morale. They overlook the various workplace forces that affect motivation and accomplishment. Sure, we should expect staff members to bring internal motivation to their jobs when hired and thereafter. More often, however, the leader should examine and even re-design the work environment features that may be triggering deflated morale.

One human performance authority says: *"The absence of performance support [not individual skills and knowledge] is the greatest block to exemplary work performance."*[11] Specific ways to overhaul elements within these two performance categories are spread throughout the book.

Things within the individual. The preeminent thinkers who created the various models for performance improvement allocate the other 10-15% of workplace performance influences to the activities occurring related to employee *Selection and Development*. Effectiveness in these realms requires, first, that leaders possess a fairly keen aptitude for hiring and matching people with the right skills and traits to the right job. If you, as

[11] Gilbert, T., in *Fundamentals of Performance Improvement*, 3rd edition. 2012, p.11 Van Tiem, D, et al.

occasionally happens, make a "poor" hire, it will feel like swimming upstream for you and the employee. Unending resources will be expended when, from the start, there was poor alignment between the job and the incumbent.

Imagine, for example, you hire someone for a client-facing, high interaction job who is not very personable. It could be that engaging people all day is neither comfortable nor enjoyable for that person; there are nice people who just aren't that interested in interfacing with people all day. Why wouldn't you know that before hiring? Did the job posting clearly describe the job functions and attributes? Did you use the right interview questions? There could be myriad reasons. Reexamine your Selection processes, and you'll better match your hires, then support them with a great work environment.

Then, there's *Development*. Be sure you provide resources and supports for your people to grow their internal capabilities and job skills. Many people come to the job with the *potential* to perform well. Yet, since they haven't held THIS particular job before, they will need some level of onboarding, mentoring, or training around processes and systems specific to the new organization. Also, skill requirements can change as the work evolves; this obligates you to plan for ongoing development.

Caveat: Note that the absence of these performance factors doesn't stop some people from producing good work. **People, especially high achievement workers, work every day**

and for years in less-than-optimal work contexts. The point is the leader can add value by thinking and acting in ways that make it easier (and more predictable) for people to be highly engaged as they produce great results.

2. Fine-tune the work setting for greater success

Now, consider how to put the model to work to build a satisfying, high achievement workplace. I usually begin consultancies (whether strategy or team development) by asking such questions as: *So, what are the values that drive the organization's culture? How does each of your roles help the organization succeed? In 3-5 years, what does the organization aim to accomplish?* In many cases, the queries are met with silence. I then remind them of some of their aspirational statements since they are critical drivers of success.

Performance factor gaps play a part in derailment: At times, when an executive is facing crisis about their performance, a quick observation reveals a discrepancy between what they and the person to whom they report saw as good performance. I proceed to ask to look at the annual goals and objectives. More times than not, they are both unclear about their meaning, thus open to misinterpretation, resulting in misaligned work. This reveals a gap in the performance factor related to clarity of goals, roles and expectations.

As a leader, awareness of the six key performance factors, in this case, should prompt you to clarify and recalibrate expectations for all parties. This joint clarity enables everyone to direct their resources towards the right work. It also allows a supervising leader to determine whether a staff under-performance situation is due to a capability or other type issue.

This framework was transformational for me. It altered how I lead and support other leaders to increase their efficacy. It's a compelling mental model to help uncover what leaders need to have in place to evoke the best performance from their people. I discovered there are many low-cost ways to enhance the work environment. What about providing the timely information people need to do to their jobs, sharing organizational goals, clarifying expectations, or procedures, or giving feedback well?

If the workplace is to be one that motivates your direct reports to produce their best work, a major part of your job is to declutter their path, i.e., remove the barriers to stellar achievement.

Improving a rather low-performing team. George inherited a team when promoted to a senior role at a consulting company. He was given license by his more senior leader to transition some of the long-tenured staff out. They weren't producing the results at the same level as their counterparts on other teams. Before doing so, he sat down with each report to hear their view of their performance, where they thought they excelled, how they'd love to get better, how they viewed their job's contributions, and finally what they needed to do their best work. He also dusted off the job description and asked them the extent to which it reflected the work they were doing.

After mining this information, George could see several ways he could ensure he removed apparent barriers to them doing their jobs well. He revamped the work environment by:

1) reacquainting them with the job description (either it needed to change some of its "essential functions", or they needed to change some of the work they were doing and the amount of time they gave to each work function).

2) Brought more specificity to their performance goals.

3) Began conducting individual coaching and goal check-ins.

4) Advocated to have support staff handle administrative tasks which consumed about 20% of their time.

5) Acted as a partner, coach and developer to help them think through their more challenging client cases and launched learning and feedback sessions to sharpen and update skills related to the services they were provided.

Over the ensuing four years, not a single consultant was terminated, and each showed dramatic improvements in their performance, level of engagement and fulfillment with the valued work they were doing.

The lesson in this case is that the absence of any performance factor means good people may be missing something that aligns, clarifies, and prompts their best performance.

When a flower doesn't bloom, you fix the environment in which it grows, not the flower.

Something to Try: Below are questions that can help you target and enhance the work environment. Think about each area and the team you lead. Then place a Y (for Yes), N (for No) or U (for Unsure) after each question.

	Work Environment Enhancement Questions	**Y, N, or U**
Goals, Roles, Expectations	1. Does the organization regularly communicate its strategic goals with staff? 2. Do staff know how their roles help achieve the org's goals? 3. Are expectations for performance clear and agreed upon? 4. Is the performance system clear, administered fairly and supportively, etc.? 5. Are job roles clearly delineated, adequately staffed, with appropriate workload, clear authority and limits? 6. Is the workflow logical and efficient?	
Coaching, Feedback & Reinforcement	1. Does the staff consistently know how well they are doing and which improvements are needed? 2. Do managers possess basic coaching and supervisory skills? 3. Does the leader have regular coaching, feedback and listening meetings with each staffer? 4. Does the manager provide feedback and support for each person that is specific, useful, constructive and educational? 5. Are the goals and priorities periodically reinforced for each staff person? 6. Are performance checkpoints scheduled throughout the year?	

Work Environment Enhancement Questions		Y, N, or U
Tools, Processes	1. Do staffers have the necessary materials and equipment to do their jobs well? 2. Is the workspace safe and conducive for work? 3. Are the job supports and procedures up-to-date, sufficient, easy to access and easy to use? 4. Are role models or mentors for the desired behavior accessible? 5. Do staffers have access to job-related experts?	
Incentives & Consequences	1. Are incentives, including pay, fair and equitable? 2. Is there an ongoing recognition system? 3. Does the non-monetary incentive system provide the type of incentives valued by the employees? 4. Does the incentive system reward the desired priority (right) behaviors? 5. Are there consequences for undesirable results? 6. Are there career advancement opportunities available as rewards for good performance?	
Internal to Individuals		
Selection	1. Do job descriptions accurately describe the "real" job requirements? 2. To what extent are the skills, functions and attributes for the job accurately described? 3. Does the selection and interview process focus on the specific and critical job requirements, along with the physical, and emotional attributes? 4. Does the work environment support the qualified individual's capacity to perform well? 5. Does the organization have or need flexible arrangements to enable the qualified individual to perform well?	
Development	1. Is there an onboarding/transition process for new hires to ensure early success and integration into the organization? 2. Are periodic skill assessments given? 3. Do employees have annual learning plans (including funding) to ensure their skills keep pace with changing job requirements? 4. Are there structured opportunities for mentoring and shadowing?	

Activity: List 1-3 specific actions you will take to enhance the workplace and enable your team to thrive. Use your responses to the questions above and prioritize the current, critical modifications. Include changes the staff will value that make achieving their goals easier and more satisfying.

1. ______________________________
2. ______________________________
3. ______________________________

In summary, knowing the interconnected system of work performance drivers makes your work easier. Remember:

> *"Over the long haul, even strong people can't compensate for a weak process. Sure, some occasional success may come from team or individual heroics. If you pit a good performer against a bad system, the system will win almost every time. We spend too much time 'fixing' people who are not broken, and not enough time fixing organization systems that are broken."*[12]

This closes Chapter 4 and Part One, written to help you take a wide view of the changing landscape within which you will lead others. A number of supportive tools related to topics in Part One are provided in **Parts Two and Three.**

[12] Rummler, G. & Brach, A., in *Exemplary Performance*, Elliott and Folsom, 2013, p. 91

Part Two

Know and Grow Yourself

"The most compelling parts of the leadership development initiative were those that focused on self-awareness. Becoming clearer about my communication and leadership style helped me adapt so I can be better with the people I lead."

—mid-level nonprofit executive

These words from a Generation X leader with whom I worked, signal that time spent in self-reflection and doing the work of shifting perspectives and building new skills can yield positive results. Focusing on your own performance and mindset can benefit the leader, those you lead, and everyone in your orbit.

Part Two asks and assists you in answering these and other questions. *Who are you as a leader? What are your beliefs that underpin how you lead others? Where are you now on the leadership journey? Where are you headed and why? How do you need to grow to get there?* To know oneself is critical to effectively leading others. It opens the space to assess, tap into, and grow your skills, allowing you to increase your capacity to lead in r-changing times.

Chapter 5 is included to help those launching into a new leadership role plan their strategy for success.

This section has five chapters:

5. Considerations for Your Launch into Leadership
6. Know Yourself: Style and Strengths
7. Know Yourself: Mindset and Beliefs
8. Grow Yourself to Grow Your People
9. Building a Synergistic Team

*It's a special privilege to be selected to lead others, one for which we begin demonstrating our worthiness for the position by **preparing** to succeed.*

Chapter 05
Considerations for Your Launch into Leadership

After years of working with first-time and seasoned leaders as they switch jobs, I'm an avid cheerleader for employing a well-planned approach to onboarding, transition and organizational integration. Having blundered a few times when bringing on new team members, I'm all in—a witness to the power of such planning. This chapter should be an early read for those beginning new leadership roles, especially if you will be leading a team of people.

The following pages explore some common themes associated with effectively leading in a new role while circumventing the various routes to derailment (Chapter 2 gives details on those patterns). These pages might be helpful to those who start out exuberant and prideful only to find that between 90 and 180 days into the role, they are overwhelmed by the sense that things are not working as well as expected.

The topics for Chapter 5 include: 1) The case for leadership transition plans, 2) Prepare your mind, and 3) Map a *better* plan to send the right signals.

1. The case for leadership transition plans

The real story below is representative of some experiences of people with whom I have worked as coach or trusted friend.

"Being selected to become the leader, chosen above all the other candidates, felt like a highlight of my work life and a boost to my personal esteem. Then, three months in, my euphoria gave way to anxiety and sleep-disturbed nights, as I wrestled with how to accomplish what the organization required of me. 'These people don't do what I need them to do!'

Undeterred, I willed myself to show them who the boss is, pressing them with mandates, reprimands, even threats. And, in case it sounds like I'm the worst boss ever, during that first year, I tried incentivizing my team's performance. There were bonuses, extra paid time off, pizza outings, and public praise.

I really worked hard with the team I inherited, but to little avail. Even the previously few cheery staff members became more aloof and gloomier. Not giving up, I told myself: 'I'll just build a whole new team. I'll even seek out a few mini-Me's-

who get it.' Best decision ever. My excitement was renewed, though it was soon dampened by how much of my time it took to get them ready for their new jobs. Feeling burdened still, I had a hard time getting to the results needed, and I again became anxious about whether I'd be able to keep the job I tried so hard to get. After six months with the new staffers, they too seemed not able to cut it. What now?

This leader can't go back and change any of these actions, but they can begin their next job differently and more strategically. They can make time to better plan their transition.

Some benefits of transition planning

It's difficult to quantify the positive difference preparing for a new role makes. Nonetheless, based on numerous experiences that saved jobs, accelerated learning, and directed the new hire to the *right* work, some of the payoffs of planning include:

- ☑ Demonstrates mature, thoughtful leadership
- ☑ Helps accelerate the time to begin achieving valued accomplishments; less time on figuring out how things work
- ☑ Avoids common missteps
- ☑ Structured, systematic method to make best use of your time
- ☑ Fosters new learning, considers strengths and blind spots
- ☑ Integrates effectively and quickly into the new culture
- ☑ Develops a thought-out plan for building direct reports' trust
- ☑ Establishes the right relationships early
- ☑ Identifies ways to achieve some early successes and in ways that matter to the organization

So, who is responsible for your transition plan?

The hiring manager, i.e., your direct supervisor, is responsible for integrating you into the organization effectively—to set you up to succeed. They are often aided by the human capital team, though transition services are typically limited to some version of an onboarding orientation. These conventional welcoming activities might include introducing you to the larger staff team, posting announcements that you've arrived, securing your work equipment, providing log-ins to systems you'll use, arranging tours of the workplace, and ensuring you complete the right paperwork to get paid on time, etc.

These functions can be satisfying activities that help you feel a part, but these are generally not the types of situations that make your leadership launch succeed or fail. Those "make or break" experiences are wholly different and require your attention. They will be outlined as you continue reading.

Don't leave it to chance. If your hiring manager doesn't have much of a plan, and many don't, take the initiative to create a plan (see page 79 for a worksheet) and work with your higher ups to refine and implement it. It will be worth it.

Another viable option is to engage a leadership transition coach or strategist to be your partner at least through your first six months on the job. Such a partner should be familiar with transition and integration priorities and can help you privately explore critical areas related to such tasks as gathering "people" intelligence, aligning and recalibrating your skills and style, and getting crystal clear on what performance looks like and your best pathways for achieving it. The partner/coach can help you build targeted action plans to be ready to succeed while making corrective steps along the way. Medium to larger organizations are more open to and encourage contracting with a coach on your behalf; they know there's a valued return on the investment.

My story bungling onboarding staffers. Like many leaders, there was a time I, too, thought once hired, people should and can just get to work. My thought was: *In the interview, you claimed you've done this before; you gave such glowing testimony of how well you did this work, so get to it.* I had, through benign neglect or because of a time crunch, not considered what specific things needed to be in place to prepare new direct reports to achieve their work goals. Some of the items I overlooked included specific onboarding plans for new hires, getting people acclimated to the organizational culture including adapting to my style, and articulating clear job segments and expectations. I wish I knew then what I know now. In any case, if all you are offered is the new employee orientation, take the initiative to create yours and follow it.

As you go through the next several pages, I have proposed a two-prong transition approach, divided into prepare your mind and map a *better* onboarding plan. A questionnaire is at the end of the chapter to help you think through many of the topics.

2. Prepare your mind

Spend time thinking about the new job and how to best get started. Consider such questions as: *Why should people follow me or even respect me as the new leader? What are the messages I want to send about who I am and how I lead? What do I hope to bring to leading this new group of people?*

As you prepare for and during your early days in your new role, you want to uncover which ways of applying your talents will play well and which won't. You can then adapt your way of thinking about how you begin your new role. Later, you may discover that some of those practices you set aside will in fact work well, but timing, attention and discernment are key.

Not all of the practices that led to your past success will be as valuable in a new setting. You will want to discover and then release these non-portable habits.

As you prepare your mind, the question of *worthiness* is one that's being explored more recently in the management field. It is also one that will help leaders, especially those who tend to demonstrate selfish ego motives, embrace a measure of humility. For others, it might mean a need to work on owning your deservedness for this higher role, particularly if you have a sense of uncertainty that is incompatible with the great talent you have meticulously accrued over the years. It can be useful to reflect on questions like these: *What makes me more worthy than the other applicants? By what right should I be in this role? Am I leading for my own gain or for a bigger purpose? And if I'm not worthy, how can I become worthy?* These can assist in resetting your mind as you step into leadership.

Acknowledge your promotion through mindset and action. One mindset adjustment is referenced in Michael Watkins' *The First 90 Days* stated as "Promote Yourself" (which in later editions, he calls "Prepare Yourself"). He shares that the newly promoted leader needs to acknowledge they are now in a completely different and higher role. He calls leaders to guard against tendencies toward attachment to their previous roles—the tasks, ways of thinking and executing.

So, one early mental shift is to make a clear, distinct break from the past role and begin identifying with the new one. It may mean choosing a specific date *(e.g., March 12 for a March 25 start date)* to mentally leave the old job behind. *What is the new level of maturity you need to begin demonstrating? What do I need to release? How will I demonstrate "I'm in a new space with new expectations requiring a new mindset?"*

3. Map a better plan to send the right signals

It's improbable that you will send all of the right signals without some deliberation. It's advisable that you focus on discovering how the depth, breadth and variations of your authentic talents can be leveraged to succeed as you move into the future. Be amenable and flexible in allowing your talents to be expressed differently in the new job.

The graphic below represents seven main areas to explore as you transition to your new position.

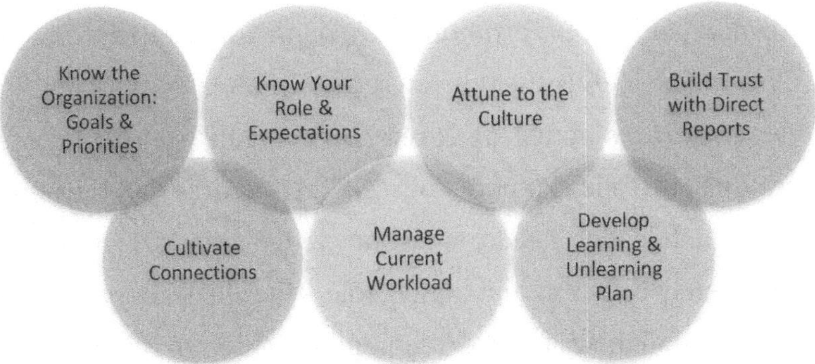

- **Know the Organization.** Before your first day, begin gathering key organizational documents such as strategic plans, goals, values, current priorities, and staff rosters. The depth of your knowledge of the organization depends on your leadership role. Regardless of your role or level, becoming familiar and somewhat fluent regarding the mission, vision, strategy and current priorities goes a long way. Find out how your role fits into the bigger plans and what value it adds to achieving the goals. Look for ways to help you learn about the organization's strengths, challenges, structure, and history. Ask questions such as: *What is everyone focused on this year? Where are we on those priorities? What have been the greatest successes over the past few years?* Basically, get acquainted with the organization to which you will be devoting a good portion of your time, your skills, and your energy.

- **Know Your Role and Expectations**. One of the biggest blunders a new leader makes is not investigating enough to grasp the expectations of their new position and how success will be measured. New leaders have been known to begin doing what they've always done without regard for what *this* new organization views as the most valuable outcomes and measures for their new position.

- **Assess and attune to the new culture:** Context matters. Devote time to learning *how things are done* and *who makes things happen*. Unwittingly, some new leaders begin losing ground at the onset of their hard-won jobs by making avoidable missteps. What they don't consider is that they are joining a pre-existing culture. Every work environment has its own peculiarities, not likely to be the same as your last one. As such, aspects of your leadership style from the last job may or may not be an easy fit in the new workplace. Then what will?

  In the early days take time to observe, reflect, and assess this new environment. Ask yourself questions like: *What kind of culture am I joining? What are the relationship styles? How do people succeed here? What are the important formal and informal networks here? How does communication happen? What's the language like here?*

Who are the influencers and key decision-makers? What's the pace of work? How do I learn to belong? What are the potential political landmines?

Derailment data indicate that of the new leaders that failed, it was not due to skill deficiency. It was more so due to poor grasp of how the organization works and cultural misfit.[13]

Pay attention to how you need to adapt to the new culture, add value, get results and become a valued change agent. Read the cultural tea leaves...early.

This doesn't mean you have to fit neatly into the culture. It suggests you need to know it, connect to it in the right way, even if your job is to reshape it to better meet the organization's needs.

As the leader, observe any cultural norms that may need to shift if they've become impediments to the organization achieving its goals. You can't leave poor cultural habits in place too long because they are quite difficult to change later without major headaches.

- **Engage and build trust with direct reports.** Presumably your top area of attention in your new role is the six to 10 people who you are directly responsible for leading. One of your first tasks with your new direct reports

---

[13] Byford, M., Watkins, M. & Triantogiannis, L., Onboarding isn't enough, HBR, May-June 2017

is to begin allaying their anxieties about reporting to a new leader, while building their excitement about the possibilities. They are, as expected, afraid or cautious; such transitions in who their direct "boss" will be produces a range of actions and emotions about how the change will impact them. Some people use this as an opportunity to exit, thinking, "I've had it. I'm not doing any more gymnastics with a new supervisor." Ask good questions, share a bit of who you are, but listen more than you talk.

(See *Chapters 9 and 12 for team development support.*)

Some first steps to connect with your new reports:

1) *Gather some background* on each direct report, such as resumes, job descriptions, tenure in role, how they've been succeeding and where they've been challenged.

2) *Meet one-on-one* with each direct report as an interested listener to learn about a) how they arrived at, get excited about, and current status of their work, b) their view of their work requirements, c) what's working well, d) where they may be challenged, e) what they need from you to deliver their best work, f) any special attributes they bring to the work and g) any questions they have for you.

3) *Plan an impressive first team meeting*. It should be well thought out since this is a first look that gives direct reports

hints at who you are and how you'll lead. (See *Chapter 9* for tips for better meetings.)

Cultivate Connections. Possessing keen organizational awareness is critical. Recognizing the main stakeholders and building relationships with them matters. This may include other leaders, peers and (in some situations) board members who have a direct influence on the job you're in. Make a list by asking yourself, *"Who are the people in my new circle that will or can have the most impact on my success?"* Inquire with the hiring manager and colleagues about who you need to know and how to prioritize them so you can plan your connecting time well.

You also want to include on your new connections list a few people who can serve as mentor or culture ambassador (those who can help you navigate the new environment) and someone doing similar work to help answer your questions. Spend lunch dates or set phone times with these key people. As you make connections, listen more than you talk; this is a connecting and learning process.

- **Manage the current workload and score some small victories:** Often, because the role you are assuming has been vacant for a long while, there's not the opportunity to exclusively spend your first 90 days transitioning, though that's ideal. Some organizations have made it a practice to have the new staffer spend their first few months getting set up, learning, connecting and assessing before taking on the normal work tasks. This gives them time to get "the lay of the land" before making major decisions. However, if there's work to be managed, it's usually best not to make drastic changes right away. Figure out what has to be done and how, then deploy your team to continue their work (making only minor tweaks in glaring situations).

Scoring some early, valued wins is also important during your first 90-100 days. Figure out how to do something effectively that matters to people and will be appreciated. Do some easy fixes, things that remove headaches or increase motivation. Streamline or improve a process that saves time for everyone, or structure better meetings if they don't exist. The point is: Find some low-hanging, valuable changes to implement early. Says leadership transition expert, Michael Watkins: "*Early wins excite and energize people and build your personal credibility. Done well, they help you create value for your new organization earlier...*"[14] This way you can simultaneously keep things moving, make changes that are additive, establish presence as a valued contributor and learn. *Think about it: What might be your early wins?*

New HR director, *too much, too fast*: This 40-something polished professional instantly began creating

[14] Watkins, M., *The First 90 Days*, 2013, page 116.

HR processes that were absent in the municipality where she began her new role. The staff was accustomed to how things have been done over the years, and they weren't used to people coming in assertively trying to change practices. These efforts to drive through change were met with strong resistance or staff interjecting enough of their "two cents" to undermine the changes. The better approach might have been to connect, include, invite, and subtly educate in order to get buy-in first—so tenured staff might feel like partners in the changes and grasp how they benefited from them. Regrettably, she was removed from the job after one year.

Note: There are situations where the new leader is hired to make sweeping changes before getting entrenched in the culture and connecting well with people. A change management strategy should be employed in this case, to manage yourself and the complexity of radical change.

- **Determine what to unlearn and learn.** Once you've got a good sense of your job, the organizational culture, expectations and goals, and your direct reports, it's time to develop a learning and *unlearning* plan. It doesn't have to be overly complicated. The plan should include quickly getting you up to speed in areas where you are under-skilled that are critical to your performance. Consider, for example, leaders who move from for-profit to nonprofit; they may be great leaders but in the new role, philanthropy becomes key. If someone was an individual specialist without direct reports and now has six direct reports, skill building in leading teams is in order.

Your plan should also help you release previously rewarding habits that might not work or which need to be applied to a lesser extent in the new role. That's *unlearning*.

A case of strategic unlearning: A new COO came from an organization that was strong on ensuring everyone was competent with systems, processes, interpersonal and facilitative skills. In his new job, he spent time learning more about financial reporting, while he put in place stronger systems for ordering, inventorying, and responsiveness to needs. He began coaching his team and helped improve the leadership meetings which, in the past, few voiced their views, and few decisions were captured.

All of these contributions raised his profile and garnered respect from his team and colleagues. He also *unlearned* that his strong drive for performance accountability didn't play as well in this more informal family-like culture. So, he pulled back on that for a while until he built enough trust with colleagues to enhance accountability in a manner that was more easily embraced.

His new learning had to do with boosting his financial acumen, for which he took an advanced course. His unlearning was summarized as slowing his super-fast pace to listen more intently and to release the assumption that the same processes that were valued elsewhere would work best. Instead, he gather more input and scaled as needed.

Contrast: Two Leaders' Approach to Similar Roles

Both became leaders of nonprofits that had some successes and myriad, urgent challenges. Both inherited long-tenured top and mid-level staff and relocated to new cities for their new CEO roles. Compare the divergent ways they began their tasks.

Leader 1	Leader 2
• Super assertive, take charge from day 1 • Told them everything they were doing wrong • Terminated long-term, loved senior staff • Insulted the board, telling them they were terrible • Rejected feedback from the board • Failed to build a network in the local community since she was an outsider	• Expressed appreciation for past work and commitment during challenging times • Clarified urgency of where the organization stood – mission goals and financial stability • Invited staff ideas on how to move forward through strategy sessions • Met with key stakeholders and peers to understand their current challenges and opportunities • Invested in building team culture and norms • Began aligning and restructuring together • Promised rewards would come if all committed to shared goals and facing the future together
Result: Board and staff shared their displeasure, and she was terminated in about one year after relocating. She may have been right in her observations, but wrong in her approach and demonstrated political naivete.	**Result:** Increased staff satisfaction, healthier culture with naysayers weeded out, staff made a part of the solution, more learning, lower-level staff promoted, attracted more donors and members

Closing Chapter 5: Thoughtfully planning your transition to a new role saves time, money and helps ensure everyone's success. This planning worksheet can help you move into your new role with excitement and an actual plan.

✓Checkpoint: Prepare to Succeed

Think about these questions, then write your responses. Skip any that have no application to the leadership role you are beginning.

Prepare My Mind

1. What are the most valuable skills, experiences and strengths I bring to my new role?
2. What 2-3 behaviors or actions does this job likely require of me that are different than in my previous role?
3. What excites me most about how I might contribute to the organization?
4. What fears or anxieties do I have and need to attend to as I begin?
5. What is the impression I hope to convey when I begin my job?
6. What practices will I use to ensure my well-being, so I keep a level head and good disposition especially during the first 60-90 days?

Culture, Priorities, Expectations

7. What information have I gathered or need to gather about the organization and its current priorities?

8. To add value to the organization, I believe the expectations and most important work priorities for me in this new role are....

9. After talking with people and reviewing organizational documents, I would describe the culture in this way:

10. What can I do to ensure I engage effectively with this culture?

Build Connections

11. Who do I need to connect with during my first 60 days and why?

Person, Dept or Orgs	Role or Value

12. My main contacts to help me become a part of the organization are:

My Direct Reports

13. What will I do with my direct reports to connect and learn about their strengths, needs, and history of accomplishment?

14. What things will I do to help bring out the best in my direct reports?

15. What might be my initial approach to leading the team given what I learned about the organizational priorities and my team members?

New Learning Priorities

16. What are 2-3 learning areas I need to pursue early to be most effective?

17. What do I need to guard against doing (unlearning) in this new role even if these behaviors or mindset were effective in previous roles?

Use this questionnaire to create your plan. Be flexible, modify it, and relax knowing you've planned for your success in your new role.

Knowing oneself should be an ongoing practice as it affirms our worth and strengths and provides insights into our next areas for growth.

Chapter 06
Know Yourself: Style and Strengths

Though most of our lives include more self-affirming than self-negating encounters, there's a tendency to gravitate to the few endeavors that are not working well. This inclination follows many people into the workplace and influences how they lead themselves and others. Leadership development thinkers (and our experiences) remind us that it's more fulfilling to build on what's working well. Terms such as strengths-based, positive psychology, and appreciative inquiry capture this idea.

Chapter 6 is directed towards assisting leaders in becoming better acquainted with themselves, especially their strengths and unique attributes. This is an initial step in optimizing your leadership skills. The topics include: 1) Self-awareness as an ongoing practice, 2) strengths, styles and competencies, and 3) putting self-knowledge to use.

1. Self-awareness, as an ongoing practice

It is *highly* advisable that leaders invest time in building self-awareness, (i.e., your strengths, style, way of engaging with people and moving through the world). Follow that up with assessing how you deploy these unique attributes at work. *Are they working for you? Are you using them in ways that lead to achieving the best results from yourself and your team?*

Why spend time on this? Setting aside time to take stock of your strengths, skills, and style offers a number of advantages. Among them are:

☑ Our naturally-occurring strengths and style can be used more effectively when we are aware of them.

☑ They can change a bit through learning and experience, and those changes may present new, unexplored opportunities to be even more effective.

☑ You can ward off the tendency to downplay or be attentive to them because they have likely become reflexive, habitual.

☑ Keen self-knowledge helps you discern when a workplace or relationship is so misaligned with who you are that they won't work. Such situations require moving so far outside of one's authentic self that great distress, even pain occur.

☑ Elusiveness about how you engage your strengths, style and skills with your employees limits your ability to name, claim and deploy your talents well (causing misjudgment, frustration, time wasting, and resistance).

☑ The higher up you go, there's a tendency to get less feedback (due to subordinates' fear of fallout based on *positional* power). Thus, seeking self-awareness matters.

☑ Paying attention to yours will help you have greater regard for the strengths and talents of others.

☑ You can ensure your strengths don't play out as weaknesses by their overuse (in settings when using them is unhelpful, i.e., when one is appreciated for directness, but at times it shows up as insensitivity).

☑ You can more confidently direct your energies to areas that allow you to soar and better deploy team members in work that is compatible with and builds on their strengths.

A Growth Story: "I'm a bulldozer." This mid-level leader came to coaching because he wanted to be a better supervisor, demonstrate better leadership presence, and grow his career. According to him, people either like him or not. He's an interesting profile—friendly, gregarious, fast-talking, youthful early 40's male. He's ready to please and driven to get into action. He ran into roadblocks with his "reach his goals at all costs" style when working with his direct reports.

We began our engagement with him completing a behavior styles profile. He loved the report and told me: "I was sitting in the airport club, and I kept chuckling and smiling as I read the profile summary – talk about spot on. So glad you had me do this!" From there, he realized, "As much as I like people, I'm actually a bulldozer."

He immediately, even before engaging in a set of informal 360 interviews with his key circle, began contemplating how he may be coming off to others and how he could improve.

The message in his story is **self-awareness has the power to accelerate change**. This self-assessment presented a composite of his behavioral style and boosted his self-insight. Then, it moved him to make some critical tweaks.

Self-awareness is one step in human development. It's even more important when others depend on us for their and the organization's way forward. Leaders and managers can use the power of their roles wisely and better by knowing themselves. Becoming increasingly self-aware takes personal reflection along with input from trusted, truthful others.

One response to the question, *What are the best leader attributes?* posed to the 67 interviewees for *The Everyday Leader* might be instructive for growth-oriented leaders. Notice that this leadership coach includes strengths, style and skills in her description, based on her consultations with hundreds of school leaders.

*"**Effective leaders** tend to be visionary, respectful, encouraging, stable, authentic, self-aware, transparent, confident, highly skilled, trustworthy and can clearly articulate goals and targets. They have a strong belief in the capacity of their team to think deeply and creatively to get the job done. These leaders understand that each member of the team brings different knowledge and strengths to the table which encourages autonomy and peer-to-peer interaction and support. They model trust through their actions and words, and they tend to be flexible, open, and consistent.*

Effective leaders are not afraid to give feedback that is clear and non- judgmental. Labeling or stereotyping others is not a part of their personality. These leaders practice personal and team accountability because they know how to grow their team." (education leadership coach)

Reflection: *How much of this description of an effective leader sounds like you?* ____________________

____

*Which words would you hope your direct reports would include when describing you?*____________________

____

Gaining a good sense of the leadership traits you are exhibiting requires deliberate reflection and gathering outside perspectives on your aptitudes and attitudes.

I've made self-awareness a lifelong practice. It's refreshing, sobering, and often fun when done with friends, trusted colleagues, and family. What this looks like for me is periodically (using both solitary and small group activities) contemplating *who I am, what makes me tick, what works for me, what doesn't, how I impact others, what matters most to me in this life stage, how I've grown over the last few years, how my perspective shifted, what I'm more and less tolerant about, and what work sends me into a state of flow and what type is more of an annoyance.* Examining these areas of identity and purpose help me bring my best to loved ones and those who I support on their leadership journey.

You may be someone who engages in self-discovery as you launch into a new year or as part of your birthday ritual. Maybe you re-set your vision and goals or pledge to embrace a different attitude. For leaders, knowing oneself is a component for your growth and efficacy, and making it a rhythmic practice will pay off. *What is or will become your practice?*

2. Strengths, style and competencies

There are three areas I believe are critical for leaders' self-knowledge, and they are interrelated. These three are:

1. ***Strengths*: These are your most dominant talents that occur naturally, successfully and repeatedly**, and for which you are better than most. There is a range of them, and they are mostly internal; a few examples—

interpersonal, analytical, empathetic, achievement-oriented, etc.),

2. ***Style*: This expresses your way of behaving and communicating.** These are more visible to others, such as extroversion, introversion, people-oriented, fast or slow paced. A few examples—gregariousness, reserved, energetic, demanding, detailed, etc.

3. ***Competencies*: These are your areas of great knowledge and skill** accrued through experience and practical learning that build on and refine your strengths. A few examples—accounting, customer service, problem solving, IT, graphic design, etc.

The worksheet on Page 92 will ask you to look at all three of these overlapping areas. For now, because it plays so much into how you show up at work, the next few paragraphs concentrate on your style –behavioral and communication.

What is your Style? There are a number of ways to heighten awareness of your style (and strengths). Ask friends, your partner, or colleagues—trusted people willing to honestly disclose. This requires asking the right questions. You can start by completing a self-administered assessment, then share with them to reveal how their view of your style aligns with yours.

Many Tools Available. There are a number of these self-administered tools. Some versions are proprietary and will cost a fee to receive a comprehensive report. Then there are simpler formats you can find for free by perusing the Internet. For my work with middle and top leaders, I recommend paying the $75 to $200 to get a more sophisticated version as these include more interpretation, recommendations, and action plans. Some options: DISC, Gallup's StrengthsFinder, Myers-Briggs, TriMetrix, and various social and emotional intelligence tools.

You can achieve *some* growth from one of these tools without any support. However, to maximize the value and accelerate progress, involve a trusted, non-judgmental partner. For confidentiality and skill at helping you explore your thinking, a formal coaching partnership often works best (even if short term), especially for those at the highest leadership levels. Also, for those who are fortunate to report to a leader who employs a coaching style, that is a good option as well.

Your Style, based on DISC. One of the widely used, simple tools for examining behavioral and communication styles is called DISC (**D**ominant, **I**nfluence, **S**teady, and **C**ompliant [Conscientious]). The thought is that each person has aspects of each of these four styles, but typically are dominated by one or two. A small set of people have just one very dominant style.

DISC has been transformative in my work with direct reports and clients. It creates a behavioral snapshot and does not give primacy to one behavioral pattern over others. Style attributes are observable behaviors (reflected in such aspects as tone of voice, emotions, body language, and pace). A person's DISC style has nothing to do with education, values, or skills. It expresses how we move through the world and engage with people of various styles. The comprehensive reports describe what environments typically work best for you, what you need to thrive, best ways to communicate with you and you with others' styles, perceptions people may hold about your style, and each style's limitations.

The presence of all four styles can add value to a work group. Extracting that value is contingent upon the leader's awareness of their and others' styles and how they can be best engaged to maximize performance in an inclusive work environment. The chart below summarizes the four main behavioral styles, as described by DISC.

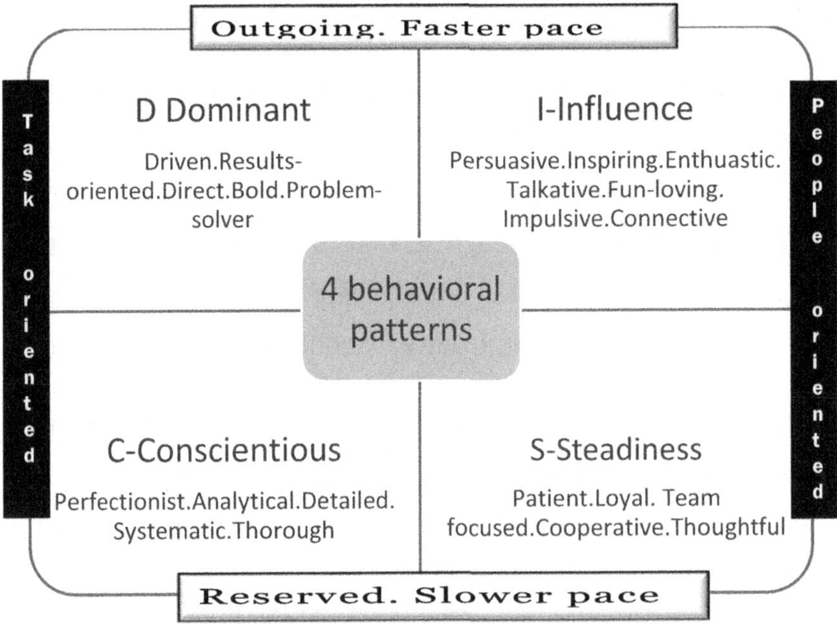

Think about your style, based on these simple descriptors for the four dominant patterns.

a) Which do you think is your dominant style of showing up and interacting? (D, I, S, or C or two)_______________

b) Why did you choose this one (or two) instead of the others?

____

____

c) What would you describe as some of the benefits of this style as a leader of your direct reports? _______________

____

____

The most profound value of self-awareness tools (DISC, MBTI or other) lies in building awareness (followed by adapting and growing) of behavioral strengths, tendencies and opportunities in your work behaviors. They create learning and taking actions in relation to areas such as your:

- Responses and tendencies during extreme stress
- Tendencies and style during conflict situations
- Team participation patterns
- Ease and challenges with other people's style
- Responses to corrective feedback
- Ways of dealing with change at work
- Habits when in situations that call for collaboration
- Emotional state when work pace accelerates

- Preferred work environment and motivators to thrive
- Managing yourself and savviness in various settings

A DISC application case. I worked with an educational leader whose DISC profile was a combination of S (Steady) and C (Conscientiousness). He was organized and process-driven when solving problems (C). He was more introverted than extroverted but was caring and concerned (S) about inclusive, collaborative decision-making, ensuring everyone felt heard. During the height of the COVID-19 pandemic, he was steady, calm and confident; he was actually energized during the crisis even as he navigated the recurring Covid surge with parents, staff and over 2000 students. He leveraged his style and other strengths, and this played exceptionally well in this high-stress situation. It helped calm the staff, allowing them to think of new ways to educate students in this unpredictable context.

Composite: Your strengths, style and skills

Imagine you are listening to someone describe you to someone else. This person has been around you a lot. They are sharing what they see as your style, strengths, and competencies. Try to visualize yourself clearly by answering these questions as bias-free as possible.

1. What do I **do well**, better than most, that comes fairly **easily**, and I find **enjoyable**? (Think about the most enjoyable aspects of your work, hobbies and things you'd do even if it was unpaid work.)

2. Notes about positive feedback I've hear consistently from people. (They might have said: "You are so good at.....")

3. Some of the ways I tend to be helpful to people... *(examples: I'm a good listener, I challenge people to do better, I lift spirits...)*

4. **Circle the 5-7 strengths that seem to best describe me....** (these are adapted from Gallup's 34 Strengths[15] themes)

Achiever Activator Adaptable Arranger Believer Command Communication Competitive Connection (to big picture) Consistency	Context Deliberative Focus Developer Discipline Empathy Focus Futuristic Harmonizer Idea lover	Includer Individualization (loves differences of others) Input Intellection (loves thinking) Learner Maximizer Positivity	Relator Responsible Restorative Self-Assured Significance Strategic WOO: (Wins Others Over)

"Each person's greatest room for growth is in the areas of his or her greatest strength..."[16]

[15] Rath, T. *Strengths Finder* 2.0, 2007

[16] Gallup.com. Strengths Revolution.

5. **Competencies/Skills:** These are the skills I've honed over years of focused learning and practical experience.

6. **Best/worst work culture features:** What aspects of the work environment work and don't work well for me?

Work culture features that are ideal for me to thrive	**Work culture features that inhibit me from thriving**

7. **During conflict or stress.** Which best describes my tendencies during conflict and high stress situations?

	Productive tendencies Ex: flexible, objective, focus on facts, empathetic, looks for causes, tactful, looks for compromises...	**Destructive tendencies** Ex: over emotional, impatient, insensitive, withdraws, defensive, personal attacks, overly critical...
During conflict		
During stress		

Next, engage another set of eyes. Once you've identified what feels right to you regarding strengths, style, competencies, and cultural features, hopefully you have at least one person who knows you, who can help confirm and even add to these lists you've created. Share and seek feedback on your self-perceptions with a trusted partner or co-worker. *To what extent do they see you the same as you see yourself? What do they see differently?*

Uncovering blind spots sometimes reminds us of unseen weaknesses but can be an inspiring awakening too. Quite often, people hear from others about blind spots that are positive attributes, areas we may have taken for granted.

Some leaders seek external views to compare with their self-perceptions by using a 360-degree feedback process. This can be done using a simple questionnaire shared with a group of leader-identified key stakeholders or by paying for a formal 360 tool (an Internet search will bring up a number of options). I have tended to be biased towards the former process. Using a short stakeholder questionnaire has yielded constructive results. (See the sample *Informal 360 Stakeholder Interview Guide* in the Appendix). This process has also had tangential advantages (especially for a leader not in the derailment mode) such as: 1) those being asked for input feeling valued by the leader and viewing their leader's engagement in the process as a demonstration of integrity, and 2) the leader is modeling to his stakeholders the desire and openness to grow.

3. Putting self-knowledge to use

Knowing oneself is not sufficient; it does not automatically prompt action. Self-awareness is the beginning of the journey, not the end. One great failing, when using self-awareness tools, is when nothing happens afterwards. This is a huge missed opportunity. Don't let the self-awareness tool become a nice-to-know at a moment in time. Engage with it in ways that lead to sustained reflection and action to better leverage your strengths and proactively pursue growth in key areas for greater efficacy at work.

The aim of the leader should be to build a plan to adopt better behaviors and attitudes; in other words, adapt your style in ways that broaden your capacity to work with a range of styles. Be intentional about becoming more expansive in your style, which will help you get the most from your talented team members, your colleagues and yourself.

I have partnered with a few leaders who interpreted the recommendations on adapting their style as being asked to relinquish their identity and authentic self. At first blush, this appears a sensible response, yet it is a reflexive, growth-avoidance viewpoint. On the contrary, leaders, who seek to remain relevant, skilled and prepared for the changing leadership environment, expand, adapt and stretch their capacity. They grow into *more* of who they are, becoming flexible with the possibilities already embedded within them.

Style assessment organizations say that people adapt their styles for two reasons: 1) stress at work in situations where the work is pushing them far outside of their style and strength zones (In this case, this should be a short-term job before it begins taking a serious toll on the person.) and 2) people adapt strategically by applying their strengths differently to achieve meaningful goals. In some cases, people work on not overusing strengths in ways that limit their success. For example: Fast paced individuals, because they value their work, might slow their pace a bit to work in an older adult setting (requiring more patience) or to work within a slower moving culture.

Reaping benefits of small style adaptation: Lisa is a high-talent, extroverted, assertive, task and process-oriented client (DISC styles D-C). After reflecting on her assessment, she built a growth plan. She learned to break or decrease her habit of putting in what she observed as her *unwelcome two cents* when nobody's asked for it, and it's not related to her job.

With just that tweak, which she labels *staying in my lane*, she is thriving in her work. Her stronger interpersonal relationships with her colleagues and direct reports probably contributed to her being promoted to a more senior level.

Practical steps to move from awareness to action:

- ✓ Build a growth plan that allows you to get the most value from your strengths, style and skills. (See the worksheet at the end of *Chapter 8: Grow Yourself*)

- ✓ Identify your own style, study it, its strengths, its benefits and the challenges it may present in certain situations.
- ✓ Examine how your style interacts with other styles to either help or inhibit the quality of relationships needed for success.
- ✓ Pay attention to whether you are more or less successful communication with each direct report.
- ✓ Try simple style adaptations, demonstrating more flexibility in ways that work better for each direct report.

Summary: The lesson of Chapter 6 is to recognize your strengths, skills and style and spend most of your energy maximizing their use. Try delegating work tasks that fall far outside of these areas of thriving to your direct reports who have better-suited, complementary skills for the tasks. Also, being clear about what doesn't align well with your strengths, skills and style when taking on a leader role can alleviate taking a job that likely won't work—one that might lead you towards that unhappy place called derailment.

Be watchful of *overusing* your strengths, because too much of a strength can be detrimental in some situations. This happens when people deploy their strengths in ways that would be best served by a different style or skillset. As we will explore in *Chapter 9: Building a Synergistic Team* and *Chapter 11: The Connect Key*, effective leaders discover and thoughtfully deploy the strengths and competencies of each direct report.

"Take time to do the hard work on the front end. Do self-assessments; learn your strengths and weaknesses. It will pay off and save headaches later." retired executive

Big Ideas to Remember. List below 1-3 ideas from Chapter 6 that resonate with you.

1.

2.

3.

This closes *Chapter 6: Know Yourself: Style and Strengths.* Next, extending the *Know Yourself* theme, Chapter 7 will guide you through probing the mindset and beliefs you bring to your work as a leader of others.

When the leader develops greater self-awareness and attends to their mindset, they enable their people and themselves to unlock potential.

Chapter 07
Know Yourself: Mindset and Beliefs

Exploring one's beliefs, mindset, biases and fears is essential to maintaining healthy self-awareness. The interplay of these aspects of your worldview and identity work in the background of everything you undertake and with the people with whom you interact. Being aware of these is key to growing and exploring new and better perspectives as you lead your team.

Look at these statements. Each reflects the speaker's beliefs and mindset. We all have beliefs; some are helpful, others not so much. The question is: Do they add value as you lead others?

She's going to be difficult.
He's too young and won't get it.
People at work are basically well-intentioned.
He's got more education than I do, so he's going to challenge me.
Older workers are more stable and reliable.
You can't be nice to your staff because they'll think you're weak.
Work should be enjoyable.

Given that mindsets and beliefs are habitual and inescapable, thus requiring deliberate effort to change, this chapter will help you examine 1) Two types of mindsets, 2) your *people* beliefs at work, 3) the effect of well-being on mindset, and 4) regenerating your mindset and beliefs for greater mastery.

1. A look at two mindsets

Mindset and beliefs matter; they're influential and highly infectious (for good or not so good). They figure into how we do everything (even if we're not consciously aware), and they are apparent in the viewpoints we hold. That's why one person can view a staff person one way, and another assess that same person quite differently. Mindset and beliefs may help explain the variance.

Basic dictionary definitions explain mindset as *your way of thinking or viewing the world*, and closely related, *belief is the mental acceptance of a concept as true.* Mindset determines how you will interpret and respond to the situations you face, and beliefs are supports for one's mindset.

Mindset is described by Carol Dweck, renowned for her work in this field, as *a perception or theory people hold about themselves.* Mindset has come to the forefront in both education and the workplace, and for good reason—since a person's mindset can either be debilitating or enhancing—with potentially lifelong effects.

Dweck identifies two mindsets: **fixed and growth**. Fixed is the most limiting type. She describes a **fixed mindset** as:

> *"People believe their basic qualities, like their intelligence or talent, are simply fixed traits. They spend their time documenting their intelligence or talents instead of developing them."* [17]

Those whose mindsets are fixed believe *either you have it, or you don't. You were born with it, or you weren't. People are set, and the mold was cast long ago. People don't change.*

"I am who I am." This was a response from an executive who had asked my thoughts about moving into a new role. I noted several strengths she might deploy right away in the new context. I also suggested she try being attentive to her typically very high energy and work pace (which sometimes exasperated others). Perhaps she would think about her audience to determine when to modulate her energy to be more in sync with the other person. The leader remarked: "I can only be me, so that's what they'll get." This fixed mindset, reactive response initially made it difficult for her to see it was not a matter of not being herself. It was about being more expansive, opening herself to explore a wider range of patterns of interacting. Coaching around loosening one's grip on their mindset can be enlightening and transformational. It was for her.

---

[17]Dweck, C. *Mindset: The New Psychology of Success*, 2006

Alternately, with a **growth mindset**, according to Dweck,

> *"People believe that their most basic abilities can be developed through dedication and hard work—brains and talent are just the starting point. This view creates a love of learning and a resilience that is essential for great accomplishment."*[18]

A growth mindset supports the idea that people possess *unlimited human potential*. This means growth is ongoing and requires resilience to embrace setbacks and try on alternatives.

Know that even as we work to embrace a growth mindset, it requires attention, throughout the work cycle, to resist fixed thinking. We live in a society that reinforces that certain people are just better than others, often based on identities related to race, gender, sexual orientation, age, or socio-economics.

"My strategies are right, and they've always worked." I worked with a leader who had been told how great he was most of his 15-year career. When he became CEO in a situation that was not easy for him to navigate, he began to despair, then became defiant with the board, insistent that doing things his way was the only way since it worked in his past. After he was involuntarily exited from the role, he began to shift his fixed mindset of enduring greatness to work on building new skills.

---

[18] Dweck, C. What is Mindset? September 30, 2015, from http://mindsetonline.com.

The story reminds us that a fixed mindset includes a belief in one's innate greatness, which can show up as inflexibility in behaving and thinking. A better choice is to applaud your perseverance, resourcefulness, and commitment to stretch and grow (a *growth mindset*) and not fixate on what worked before.

The two-mindset model looks like this:

	Fixed Mindset	**Growth Mindset**
Viewpoint	*Belief that my intelligence, personality, style are set; so, spends time protecting and defending; potential is set which leads to desire to "look smart" and the following...*	*Belief that my intelligence, personality, style can be developed continually; potential is unlimited, which leads to a desire to grow and the following...*
Challenges	Avoids	Embraces
Obstacles	Gives up easily	Persist in the face of setback
Effort	Sees as fruitless	Views as path to mastery
Criticism	Rejects useful (corrective) criticism	Learns from criticism
Others' success	Feels threatened by others' success	Finds lessons and inspiration from others' success
Results	May plateau early and achieve less than capable	Reach higher levels of achievement and has a greater sense of free will

Activity: Check Your Mindset

For each A or B set below, **circle** the ones that best reflect your general mindset. Be honest with yourself.

Fixed (A)	or Growth Mindset (B)
1. This is too hard.	This will be challenging but I'll keep working on it.
2. People don't change.	With effort, people can change habits.
3. I am just naturally good at this.	I am working hard at this.
4. Failure means I'm at the limits of my ability.	Failure is an opportunity to grow in new ways.
5. They are just naturally smarter than I am.	I'm on the right track.
6. I've never been good at this anyway.	I'm going to think through this more carefully.
7. I quit.	I'll try a different approach.
8. I'll never learn it.	I'll take a fresh look tomorrow.

# of A responses ______ **# of B responses** ______.

My biggest struggle with a fixed mindset is apparent when: ____

____

2. Your *people* beliefs

Mindset and beliefs are inevitable, a part of life. Our work is to be aware of them and how to use them to be the best leader we can for those who follow us.

Beliefs form over time. Generally we develop them 1) through lessons we are taught as truths (parents might say: “do good to others, and they’ll do good to you” or “you’re not as good as your sister”), 2) accrued through our own experiences (“everything will work out” or “people will undermine you, so don’t trust them”), or 3) by examples (you might mimic a previous manager’s approaches and interactions with direct reports as if these are the only right ways to lead).

What beliefs (*concepts or ideas you hold as true*) form the foundation of your mindset? Building awareness of your beliefs about people and the workplace can help you be more effective. Beliefs come into the workplace with you; they are formed even before people show you who they are. You don’t leave home without them.

People can or people can’t? People will or people won’t? If your work experience has somehow soured you a bit on people, you likely bring beliefs that make it hard for people to win in your eyes. Conversely, if you were raised to view people through the lens of human worth, potential, and generally well-intentioned, you bring these beliefs to work, and they can serve you well as a leader and in some cases lead to naïve choices.

***They can't do it without us* belief.** I recall a session when I joined a group of consultants whose job was to serve as strategic partners with the organization's leaders. During my first meeting, it struck me that the majority of the 35 consultants believed wholeheartedly that the leaders *needed* them to run their operations; in fact, they stated, the leaders were not smart enough to do it without them. A few challenged that argument, suggesting that with a bit of support, the leaders can be effective without constant hand-holding from the consultants. This could free the consultants to spend time increasing the capacity of others. "No, you don't understand; they can't do it without us." They held firm in their *belief* that these leaders were incapable of improving, thus the leaders needed the consultants' constant monitoring and rescuing.

When considering mindset and beliefs, astute leaders strive to carry out their work premised on constructive *people* beliefs--views that expand rather than limit possibilities. There are, unfortunately, plenty examples of leaders holding negative beliefs about people that taint how they lead direct reports.

The autocratic, top-down, punishing-type paradigm comes out of a certain set of beliefs about people and how they are motivated to perform. Often this approach is deeply rooted in the leader's unexplored fears—such as fear of losing control, of being exposed, of not being confident, of not feeling skilled, and more. And those fears, too, are rooted in some largely unconscious limiting beliefs held by and about the leader.

The *New York Times*, during summer 2021, reported that Amazon founder and CEO, Jeff Bezos, tracks his workers every move because he believes people are inherently lazy.[19] Consider the kind of workplace culture this perpetuates. Does this really lead to higher performance, high employee retention and satisfaction? That's doubtful. Belief influences culture.

What's the leader's underlying belief in this story? *"My most frustrating experience was having a supervisor who was critical and focused very little on what was right, but rather what was wrong. This supervisor hardly ever even gave a simple compliment. But when they did, they'd tag it with, 'but that's your job'."* –Interviewee, talent management executive

Our beliefs influence our *interpretation* of the events and situations we face, even more so than the actual events or situations. These beliefs we each hold are about ourselves, about other people, and about the world and how it works.

As leaders, one of our tasks is to think about the extent to which our beliefs are helping or harming our effectiveness with those we lead. Many of your beliefs have and continue to help you succeed; others may need to be re-imagined.

Awareness is the key to dismantling or altering an unhelpful belief system (pg. 55) [20]

---

[19] The Amazon that customers don't see. June 15, 2021.

[20] Paterson, R. J. *The Assertiveness Workbook*, 2000, pages.54 and 55

People Beliefs: Take a moment to consider your beliefs about people in the workplace. **Do any of these 20 people beliefs resonate with you? Indicate Y (Yes), N (No) or M (Maybe) for each one.**

Belief statements	Y, N, M
1. People need some autonomy and empowerment to do their best work.	
2. The people I lead belong to me; I'm the boss, they're my subordinates and should fall in line behind me.	
3. I don't need to compliment people for doing what they are supposed to do; the paycheck does that.	
4. People will try to get away with whatever they can, so I have to supervise closely.	
5. Taking time to learn and develop is fluffy stuff that takes away from doing the work.	
6. I trust that people want to do a great job, so my job is to provide the support to help them do that.	
7. If people disagree with me as the leader, it means something is wrong with me.	
8. Staying busy with many tasks is an important indicator that I am dedicated to the job.	
9. People are generally capable, committed, and want to do a great job.	
10. If I'm not aggressive, people will run over me and not do their work.	
11. Most people don't believe in the organization and only work to get a paycheck.	

12. I believe in the dignity and worth of each person.	
13. Everyone on the team can learn and grow.	
14. I believe people are generally out for themselves.	
15. People deserve the best, supportive environment when they come to work.	
16. People are always waiting for others to fail.	
17. It's people's own fault if they leave work feeling stressed and anxious.	
18. A happy work environment is a sign of weakness.	
19. People should have time for work, home and recreation.	
20. Others (list any others of your own)...	

What 1 or 2 beliefs do I need to adopt to be more effective leading and working with others?

____

____

____

____

____

3. Effects of well-being on mindset

Well-being habits affect your mindset, and mindset affects the quality of your leadership. Even with a growth-oriented, strengths-based style and mindset, without habits that keep you centered, refreshed and grounded, your strengths will play out in less-than-optimal ways.

People tend to underperform and make uncharacteristically poor decisions and blunders when they are experiencing diminished wellness and overall low-quality well-being. When you're in states of high stress, haven't had enough rest, have lapsed into poor physical wellness habits, or are contending with personal or emotional concerns, it can affect how you bring yourself to work. Your mood and temperament have a bearing on those around you, especially your team members.

What do you do to get back to your center, to balance? How do you find your still point and regenerate yourself? What are your well-being practices? And to what extent do you inquire about and foster the same with your direct reports?

There's a tendency for leaders to steer clear of talking with team members about their well-being, yet the extent to which they or you attend to them shows up in the work you each do. When you aren't physically or emotionally prepared to bring the best of who you are to your work, the wellness depletion gremlin can show up instead and wreak havoc on everything and everyone you touch, disappointing yourself and others.

Well-being practices are increasingly a consideration for workers and even more so for leaders because the cost of a leader's mistakes reverberate more widely. Consider for yourself and your staff the state of what Gallup[21] describes as the five key areas of well-being:

1. **Career Well-being:** Satisfaction and enjoyment with your work
2. **Social Well-being**: Having meaningful friendships with regular contact
3. **Financial Well-being**: Success at managing your financial resources
4. **Physical Well-being**: Experiencing a condition of physical wellness through a healthful lifestyle
5. **Community Well-being**: Finding pleasure in living where you do

A wellness lesson learned: The client admitted he was moving much too fast, not sleeping or attending to his partner at home. "I feel like a monster sometimes at work. It's not who I am, but I'm driving everyone crazy at work and home." After

[21] Gallup.com. 10 Well-being practices to guide leaders. 5/7/2021.

a few coaching sessions, better practices began to emerge. As he explored his goal of being a more effective supervisor, it became clear this was connected to attending to his well-being. As he began applying strategies to address his personal concerns, he got back on track and discovered better ways to use his skills. He's calmer, while still passionate; he's practicing techniques to find stillness and reset his frantic pace. He slowed down enough to attend to coaching (rather than firing off orders) his direct reports. They are happier and productive and so is he.

4. Regenerating your mindset for greater mastery

Below is a comparison of two leader/manager mindsets in action. Notice the fixed versus growth mindset differences. Where are you most situated? Review the chart and identify 1) areas where you are already thriving and 2) one area where you may need to make some shifts to enhance your leadership.

Boss-Leader Style *Fixed Mindset* →	**Coaching-Leader Style** *Growth Mindset*
General Description	
Leader takes on each direct report's challenges and responsibilities and becomes the hands-on leader of every situation, fostering dependency on the leader	*Leader uses their position to uncover information about the system and culture that team members can use to resolve their problem. Direct reports gain confidence in and use of their own resources.*

Boss-Leader Style *Fixed Mindset* →	Coaching-Leader Style *Growth Mindset*
Contrasting Beliefs	
People cannot solve problems or create without your constant involvement.	Direct reports can come up with approaches that work for them, rather than adopting your solutions.
You must look over team member's shoulders because they are likely to blow it.	People are resourceful and capable of growth.
You are certain you would do a better job than team members, so you act in ways that create passivity.	Good enough solutions and actions by committed team members are developmental and will lead to even better results over time.
Contrasting Behaviors	
You focus on team members' weaknesses.	You spend more time on team members' strengths.
You make all the decisions for team members.	You seek chances to invite team members to be decisive and articulate those decisions.
You take up more airtime than your staffers when you are with them. They learn more about you than about each other.	You invite team members to share ideas and collaborate with work mates to enhance work outcomes.
You spend more time speaking, making assumptions, and giving directions.	You spend more time observing, listening, asking questions, and inviting thinking and processing.
You assign blame.	You help staff accept responsibility.
You give the plan and tell your staff to follow it.	You support direct reports in developing or co-creating their work plans.
You act as if work is life; all time is work time.	You bring a refreshed mind and body to work, ready to make the best impact on people and the goals.

Know Myself Activity: Biggest takeaways

Take a few moments to jot down your thoughts on the six items below. Maybe you will restate what you've noted from Chapters 6 and 7, or you can build on those reflections to create a snapshot that helps shape your leadership pathway.

1. My mission as a leader is to……

---

2. My general style is….

---

3. My strengths are…..

---

4. My beliefs to support my mission are….

---

5. My well-being practices include…..

---

6. My growth areas include….

Next. Now that you've worked through Chapters 6 and 7 to get in touch with your strengths, skills, and beliefs, the next chapter helps you put these assets to work and add a few new competencies. Chapter 8 explores ways to propel forward as you stretch and Grow Yourself.

The idea that we can maximize human potential opens the way to an exciting, unending journey for boundless progress.

Chapter 08
Grow Yourself to Grow Your People

I've occasionally heard leaders reference their educational credentials as evidence of their skill and qualifications to be successful in their role. Often, these credentials were earned a decade or more ago, and the leader continued applying the same practices over those years—doing little to sharpen their skills. Astute leaders anticipate transformation in the work environment, which necessitates acquiring new learning for continued efficacy. Or, as Marshall Goldsmith's book title declares *What Got You Here, Won't Get You There.*

Chapter 8 supports you in actualizing continued development as an exciting aspect of your leadership journey. The chapter emphasizes the link between a leader's commitment to ongoing growth and their direct reports' dedication to continued growth and higher performance. This chapter suggests six specific and powerful strategies you can adapt to your needs to enhance your capacity to lead others more effectively. These six are: 1)

Build your support network 2) build on strengths and inner resources, 3) uncover and attend to blind spots, 4) improve your emotional intelligence, 5) align your leadership presence, and 6) execute targeted learning plans. Before delving into those strategies, the chapter starts by looking at the *power* and ripple effects of your ongoing development.

The power of continuous growth

So, why should you have a growth practice? By now you know that leader development is a pressing and rewarding matter with ripple effects on your direct reports, colleagues and the organization. Growing your skills to keep pace with the needs of the changing environment also makes sense. Finally, people often never move beyond awareness of their need to grow. *Knowing* (i.e., awareness) is not doing, not growth itself; it's a first step in giving attention to the often-neglected development of supervising leaders. The simplified change process (depicted on the right) means leaders must be motivated enough to act on their awareness to achieve, engage and sustain new learning.

Awareness
Urgency (Motivation)
Actions
Sustain Growth

The leader role is imbued with power. Own it, then learn to use it wisely. An early consideration is acknowledging the ***power*** inherent in your role. A leader, at whatever level, influences people, situations, and outcomes, just by virtue of the position. Whether the leader possesses the talent commensurate with the role's requirements, their voice and actions count for more than if they were not the leader.

For example, I've witnessed the adverse effect of unskilled board chairpersons on an organization. They run board meetings like their personal fiefdoms and push through decisions that can lead to long-term harm. Other scenarios are those where staff members fall in line behind their leader's bad behaviors and decisions, silently waiting it out until the power-abusing leader is removed or leaves on their own.

The abuse or misuse of a leader's *power* with direct reports is a major complaint and source of suffering among those in their charge. It is often a cover-up for an insecure leader, one unsure of their worthiness to be in the role. Here are responses from a few interviewees about the impact of an ineffective manager.

"I work long hours because we are short staffed, it's tough. And the manager talks to me like I'm nothing, nobody." (housekeeping staff for a residential facility)

Under one leader, I lost my voice for a few months; I felt unheard, oppressed. I entered speech therapy. Since I left that organization, I haven't had that problem. I did however, for a time, question my abilities; I felt unable to speak up for myself. Now after several years, I am more confident. (anonymous)

I was told 'don't forget that I sign your check!' That was a threat. That was disrespectful. That was intimidation, and a weak one at that for me, who has always believed that I will succeed, somewhere, someway. It was a way to stop dialogue, not encourage it. It diminished my respect for that person. (Interviewee, retired senior leader)

Not all leaders misuse the power inherent in their role, and it is reassuring to hear about praiseworthy supervisors. These leaders create workspaces where staff feel valued and engaged and have an additive effect on their team members' life quality. Studies consistently report that having *great managers leads to higher staff performance, satisfaction and retention.*

She connected me to the other staff and gave me a seat at the table. She communicated goals, gave clear timelines, and set expectations. She suggested ways to accomplish the work to get me started but allowed me to figure out the style that worked best for me. We would troubleshoot together. I loved working with her and did an outstanding job. (nonprofit project intern)

As the leader, I trusted that the knowledge of the team was greater than mine when trying to select the HRIS systems. I let them set the schedules, and they invited me to the meetings, not to watch them, but because they were proud to show their achievements and I was honored to be asked. We need to trust we have hired talented people and let them do their work. (Interviewee, EVP, Human Resources)

Don't conflate compliance with staff satisfaction. Polling organizations consistently report that leaders' perceptions of how well they are doing diverges greatly from their direct reports' views. *"I'm doing well with all of my direct reports; I've never heard them say differently."* If you find that a number of your staff members are silent, compliant, or passive in team or individual meetings, don't assume they are satisfied, thriving employees. Some have resigned themselves to how you deploy the weight of your role and chosen compliance as their *get along* strategy that enables them to tolerate what may be an unfulfilling setting to keep their paycheck coming.

Think through how you may be impacting the people who report to you. Review the beliefs you hold that may make work easier or more taxing for them. Also reflect on your style attributes that inspire your direct reports to give and produce their best. Then complete the activity below.

Activity: My Effect On My Direct Reports

Instructions: Place the initials of each direct report in the first column. Then use simple words to describe 1) their general disposition at work in relation to you (use adjectives- upbeat, uptight, laid back, intense, etc.) 2) your habits that seem to have an additive (+) effect on them and 3) those that seem to hinder them from being their best. If you can't answer, begin paying attention as a first step, then come back to this.

Initials	Disposition	My + habits	My – habits

As you grow, others will too. As an influencer and model, as you begin to demonstrate greater skill in engaging people, you will discover it's infectious. Positive behaviors can be just as infectious as poor behaviors, hopefully even more so. As you use your voice, influence and talents to articulate and exhibit values and viewpoints that affirm what constitutes a healthy, thriving workplace, these will catch on among your staff team and colleagues.

As you display new levels of maturity and humility, the practices for *best managers* identified by the 67 interviewees will come to life as well. Here are a few of the items from Chapter 1: The best managers...

- Let their people know their position is important and valued.
- Inspire their team around a vision.
- Have high expectations and holds self and team accountable.
- Advocate for their staff members.
- Are open to diverse people, thoughts and ideas.
- Focus on both the organization and the staff.

Owning your power builds agency and reduces blaming. When faced with setbacks or major blunders, one reflexive leader response is to blame other people or something outside of themselves. "*They, He, She, It... caused my poor results.*" "*If I had better people.*" "*The board was blocking my way.*" "*My colleagues sabotaged me.*" These are all statements that externalize your situation and diminish your agency to take responsibility and make changes.

I've engaged several coaching clients who started off deflated about a work failure and commenced to vent about the people and situations that caused things to go wrong. I then steered them from externalizing to owning responsibility, allowing them to claim their power to act in ways that could yield better results. *What role do you feel you played in this situation that landed you here? If you could go back, how might you approach it? What did the setback teach you? What can you take from this to move into the future better and stronger?*

I've observed clients stepping back from such scenarios, then allowing themselves to own up to their challenges. Thereafter, they acted as self-correcting, self-generating leaders. This always re-affirms my belief in the human capacity to change.

Change strengthens a marriage. One client shared: *"This self-work has helped my marriage, although that wasn't our purpose. My partner said, 'Wow, I notice you are responding better to our issues. I feel heard. You are calmer when we have problems, even saying things like, 'that's on me.' I like that."*

> *"Quite simply, in any human group, the leader has maximal power to sway everyone's emotions...how well leaders manage their moods affects everyone else's moods, which becomes not just a private matter, but a factor in how well a business will do."*[22]

Six Growth Strategies

What follows are six actionable approaches to move from knowing to growing yourself. These are merely a sampling of

[22] Goleman, D. *Primal Leadership*, 2002.

actions that have proven transformational and achievable by those committed to their development.

1. Build your support network

This first strategy is fairly straight forward and can produce meaningful results if your network is comprised of the right people with the right qualities. Belonging to a network of trusted connections can affirm your success, help you see blind spots, help you think through testy issues, challenge you to explore various perspectives, and connect you to others.

Sharing and learning with and through others is a low-cost investment and has little to do with gratuitously passing out business cards. It means building authentic circles of relationships where there's real reciprocity—sharing and caring, learning and giving, making time, and being present for each other. Many enriching connections are developed organically, simply by paying attention to strengths and attributes of those around you, in formal and informal settings.

A better network: In the space below jot down a few names or groups for your network of people who can...

☑ Provide knowledge, resources and insight about your specific industry or role.

____

____

____

☑ Offer perspectives about the culture of the organization and any landmines to watch out for.

____

____

____

☑ Serve as honest, trusting, challenging confidantes who know you well and with whom you can talk about opportunities and anxieties.

____

____

____

☑ Be cheerleaders to keep you motivated; they may not be the best for problem-solving as they are deliberately biased towards keeping you uplifted.

____

____

____

☑ Act as thinking partners to help you process your goals.

____

____

____

Where do you get the people? You can build these networks, sometimes referred to as a personal board of directors by including people such as a partner/spouse, best friends, work colleagues, or peers in outside organizations. Also think about board memberships or professional organizations, a leadership coach, and those well-connected within the organization.

A case of being poorly networked. A high-talent leader had trouble getting hired into a new role. He prided himself on his smarts, business acumen and accomplishments. He gave little attention to people who didn't impress him. When he needed to move to his next role, after restructuring eliminated his position, he shared his resume with me in response to C-suite openings (in a national organization) after not being hired for several roles he'd sought.

I asked: *Who can provide you with some intelligence to better frame your application? Did you get feedback from anyone about your interviews? Who are your advocates and champions (within the national organization)?* His response: "I don't know." He soon realized "I have no advocates or deep relationships in the network of influence. I'm not known where it matters, and I'm not in control of the messages about me."

I believe he learned that networks and collaboration matter more than he'd previously thought, and that people don't have to be on your *level* of smarts to value and connect with them. Personal expertise is often insufficient. After being out of work for a few months, he did land a great C-suite role (though not inside the national organization).

Consider a coach in your network. While leadership coaches may not be accessible to everyone, increasingly organizations see the return on investing in these confidential, thinking partners. So, consider a coach as part of your professional development plan.

Coaching clients have surprised themselves with the growth they experienced after just six months of targeted goals and a guided coaching process. They experience growth so quickly because few leaders spend a dedicated hour every few weeks self-reflecting and holding themselves accountable to make real progress on their development journey. Leaders are busy managing the endless daily challenges, and coaching may offer the structure motivated leaders need to systematically grow.

"*I feel like a new person in just six months*" remarked a client who had gotten stuck as the organization began changing expectations. She was able to think through new goals that inspired her, clarify why she felt stuck, choose actions to get unstuck and overall elevate her public stature in ways that aligned with the smarts she brought to the job. Six months was all it took, though we spent six more months on maintenance.

Testing one's thinking with a coach can save a lot of regrets. Engaging a coach doesn't imply you aren't talented; it means you are insightful enough to acknowledge "I can't see the whole picture all of the time because I'm in it and may be blinded by my own views." In reality, proactive coaching is far more effective than enlisting a coach after you've made near-fatal blunders. I have a set of long-term clients, and we explore a range of topics that come to the foreground while leading others. A few are listed below (See *Appendix* for more coaching topics for the leader or with direct reports).

1. Improve management style with direct reports
2. Identify and magnify my important strengths at work
3. Grow self-awareness; reveal things I should know
4. Improve communication and better handle conflict
5. Think and act with greater creativity and innovation
6. Adapt my style to embrace ambiguity and frequent change

Assembling the *right* people for your network can make a vast difference in your leadership. Some leaders have neglected this strategy or relied upon network members who provided unhelpful, even ego-gratifying advice, not worth emulating.

2. Build on existing strengths and inner resources

To grow... *"We simply accept our talents and refocus our lives around them."*[23]

You can become a resource-rich leader by cultivating your strengths and inner-resources. You've already uncovered your strengths by working through Chapter 6. Refer back to the activity *Your strengths, style and skills* to recall your areas of greatest talent and skill. Your growth begins by examining how these might be more strategically applied to how you lead.

---

[23] Buckingham, M. and Clifton, D., *Now, Discover Your Strengths*, , 2001, pg. 45

I encourage people to tap into the well of inner resources we each possess if they want to boost their capacity. Internal attributes such as will, determination, energy, persistence, and hope are crucial to becoming self-generating problem finders and problem solvers.

You can go a long way by developing these internal muscles and qualities, rather than focusing largely on "If only I had more of this and that... staff, sales, fees, loans, money, grants, time, buildings, transportation, technology, etc." Though tangible resources are essential for organizations to thrive, chasing after them ought not occupy all of your energy. These external resources actually become easier to acquire as you spend time cultivating the set of no-cost resources—those within.

There are deep wells of strength that are never used. –unknown

Activity: Tap into Your Inner Resources

✓Place a checkmark beside those that will take you further if cultivated. Include a few in the Learning Plan at the end of this chapter.

Creativity ____________	Energy _______
Self-Discipline __________	Tolerance_______
Confidence ____________	Composure _______
Intelligence ____________	Attitude _______
Determination ________	Passion _______
Courage ____________	Awareness _______
Hope ____________	Judgment _______
Knowledge________	Insight _______
Other? ________________	**Other?**___________________

What low-cost strategies can you use to develop two of those you identified?

1.

Action to enhance it:

2.

Action to enhance it:

---

3. Uncover and attend to possible blind areas

We all have areas of blindness, and that should not be a surprise. Our eyes aren't built to see everything. In our everyday field of vision, there is a blind spot. Simply defined, *blind spots are areas that are blocked from a person's view.*

To increase our capacity entails acknowledging there are aspects of ourselves we can't change alone because they are outside of our conscious awareness. Such areas might involve one's *unconscious biases and beliefs, idiosyncrasies, well-worn habits, viewpoints and values, instinctive response patterns, emotional messages, body language, skill level, etc.*

Areas of blindness are not necessarily related to deficiencies since people can be oblivious to their strengths too. On several occasions, young leaders recounted being surprised and uplifted by positive feedback they received about specific, valuable skills and qualities they demonstrated. They had been going about their work unaware of how prevalent these strengths were showing up to others. If you are blind to your traits and behaviors, whether good or bad, they can be self-limiting, i.e., hinder you from using these traits in the best way.

We simply can't fully observe ourselves in the same way we observe others. Think of times you later realized you had spinach in your teeth at a meeting, but no one told you. *Well, darn, I wish I had known it was there or that someone had told me so I could have fixed it; instead, I've been walking around looking silly all day.*

A Dale Carnegie White Paper of 2017[24] identified four major leader blind spots, situations in which leaders believe they're pretty good, but employees report great deficiencies. The four were delineated as follows: *showing appreciation, truly listening, admitting when wrong, and being honest with themselves and others.*

A few ways to help you gain *sight*: First, put yourself into a Growth Mindset to be ready for a bit of feedback that could run counter to your self-perceptions. Then act on external input and conduct a *personal* SWOT analysis.

[24] Dale Carnegie & Associates, Inc. Recognizing Leadership Blind Spots, wp_050817

a. Act on external input. In Chapter 6, I referenced finding people and using 360°-type assessments, either formal or informal, to see yourself more clearly. Take this information and create a plan to act on these new insights about your strengths and opportunities.

b. Conduct a personal SWOT analysis. This popular organizational tool that examines *Strengths, Weaknesses, Opportunities and Threats* can be immensely helpful when applied to an individual leader. Use it to summarize what you uncovered from chapters 6 and 7 to know yourself along with what the job and your direct reports need from you.

Instructions for personal SWOT: Fill in the four boxes below based on what you know about yourself as a result of reflection and others' input.

STRENGTHS (what I do well, talents, skills, gifts, and attributes that will help me achieve my goals)	*WEAKNESSES (important personal/internal characteristics or competencies that might interfere with achieving my goals)*

OPPORTUNITIES (developments happening or will happen in my environment or networks that could help me succeed)	*THREATS (external circumstances that might keep me from succeeding if I don't address them)*

Next, make meaning of the SWOT.

Personal SWOT Reflection & Action Questions

1. How can I better engage my strengths to achieve results?

2. What actions will I take to make progress on 1-2 opportunities?

3. Which 1-2 items identified as a weakness or threat might have the greatest impact on my leadership over the next 6-12 months?

4. Think about, and talk to a confidante, about ways to mitigate or address those specific weaknesses or threats beginning within the next 30-60 days. Write them here.

Use this SWOT for further reflection, and then integrate into your learning plan in Strategy 5 of this chapter.

4. Improve your emotional intelligence (E.Q.).

Since Daniel Goleman published *Emotional Intelligence* in 1985, E.Q. assessments have been widely used to examine a set of workplace and life skills. E. Q. expands the definition to what it means to be smart. It describes the extent to which a person is *able to perceive, use, manage and handle emotions*. Goleman extended E.Q. by illuminating the human drive for connection and sociability, with his 2006 publication of *Social Intelligence, The New Science of Human Relationships*.

E.Q. assessments can be easily located on the Internet. They help you identify and lean into your areas of exceptional emotional and social talent and also reveal your zones of vulnerability that effect your leadership. If you're wondering whether growing your E.Q. should be a priority, here's a list of indicators that may create more urgency for you to improve.

Some Behavioral Signs of Underdeveloped E.Q.

- ☑ Emotional Outbursts–overblown and uncontrollable
- ☑ Pattern of turning attention to yourself..."I, I, I..."
- ☑ Always taking credit for any success, even others'
- ☑ Emotions get in the way of working through challenges
- ☑ Low empathy towards others (out of tune, poor timing)
- ☑ Blaming others for your own problems
- ☑ Lack of emotional resilience during challenges
- ☑ Obliviousness to others' feelings
- ☑ Overly self-critical

- ☑ Poor interpersonal relationships
- ☑ Hard time reading the political landscape at work
- ☑ Need to be *right*

Have you received feedback in any of these areas? Then, they are likely areas for your attention and growth.

Here's a four-quadrant E. Q. model with related competencies.

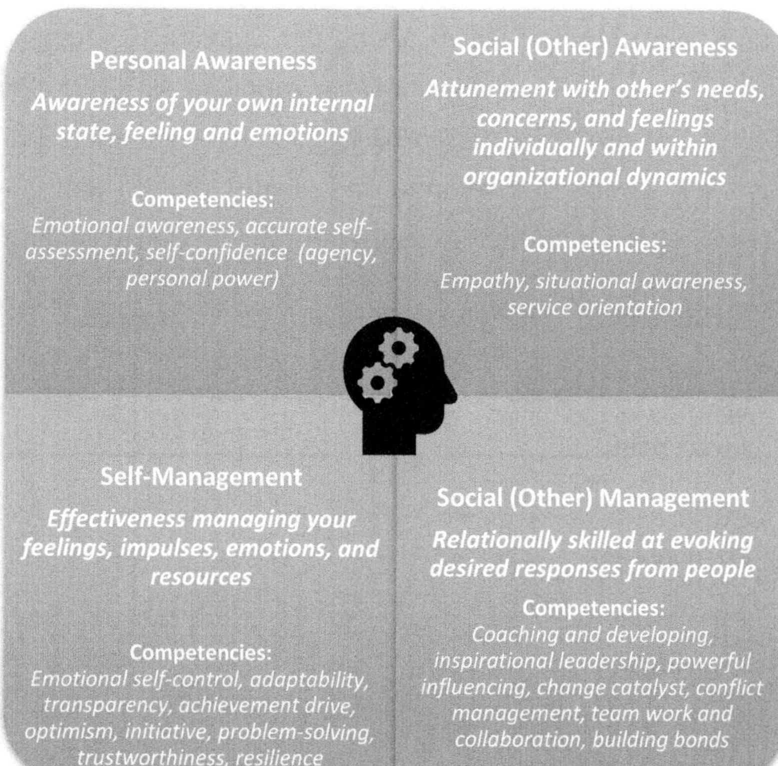

Personal Awareness
Awareness of your own internal state, feeling and emotions
Competencies:
Emotional awareness, accurate self-assessment, self-confidence (agency, personal power)
Social (Other) Awareness
Attunement with other's needs, concerns, and feelings individually and within organizational dynamics
Competencies:
Empathy, situational awareness, service orientation
Self-Management
Effectiveness managing your feelings, impulses, emotions, and resources
Competencies:
Emotional self-control, adaptability, transparency, achievement drive, optimism, initiative, problem-solving, trustworthiness, resilience
Social (Other) Management
Relationally skilled at evoking desired responses from people
Competencies:
Coaching and developing, inspirational leadership, powerful influencing, change catalyst, conflict management, team work and collaboration, building bonds

These self-assessments are generally fee-based. To get the most from them, use a trusted confidante or coach to review and determine if their perceptions are aligned with yours. These reports can also help you build a plan to make the best use of your areas of great intelligences. Select a few areas to target, those with value to your work, and begin enhancement actions.

Activity: Begin exploring your E.Q. Ask yourself whether you feel you are strong or aspirational in the four EQ areas, two related to how *intelligently* you know and *manage yourself* and two related to how *intelligently* you know and *manage others.* Using the chart on the previous page, review the competencies that support each of the four areas. List up to two (2) from each quadrant where you feel you are very strong (left column) and identify one (1) that your direct reports may think you need to strengthen (right column).

Quadrant	My Very Strong Competencies	Priority Competencies to Strengthen
Self-Awareness		
Self-Management		
Other Awareness		
Other Management		

It's not unusual that the more controlling, externalizing, and bossy the leader, the lower the level of competence in the social (other) management quadrant, especially building bonds, teamwork and inspiration. Conversely, leaders driven by a vision and who work to become the best they can be for those they lead tend to possess heightened self-awareness and other awareness. In the latter case, part of the work is to become aware of these strengths and create plans to deploy emotional agility to the greatest benefit of the team and organization.

Enhancing personal power was a game changer. *"After reviewing my E.Q. report, I was pleased to see overall I am pretty strong. An area I had not considered was Personal Power. My score was average on that, so I began to explore it and act on some suggestions in the report to elevate my personal power. I'm secure in my smarts but lacked confidence to speak my truth unless I got angry, which is ineffective. I began observing how I engage in meetings, my voice quality and where and how I speak up. I feel more powerful when I do these things, and I sense my display of personal power better matches my smarts."* –HR professional

5. Align your leadership presence

Another area that has proven beneficial to many leaders is paying attention and making shifts to how they show up with others. Leadership (or executive) Presence is a popular phrase often described in superficial terms such as wearing business attire, voice pitch, and even physical stature. However, when we are being our genuine and authentic selves, this sense of presence takes us on our own unique path. *Leadership presence is mostly about how you show up to and with others—the observable signals you send to others.*

Many new and senior female leaders benefit from investigating this concept. Given the societal norms and gender biases women contend with, there's an uneasiness about how they project competence and confidence. I have worked with such clients whose real, even exceptional, talents are under-represented or misaligned with their public presence style.

The basic questions to you are: *How are you showing up? How do you make others feel? What is your general temperament when present with people? How effective is your speaking and non-verbal demeanor? What messages are you sending, and are they representative of you as a leader? In meetings, are you conveying what you intend? What's keeping you from demonstrating your talents and skills confidently? Where is the variance between others' perceptions and your own truth?*

An example of poor presence: *"One of my most challenging experiences was working with a supervisor who was extremely moody. I never knew how things would turn out from day to day. The whole team walked around on eggshells. This affected morale and attendance. Team members would take days off quite often to avoid the tension and uncertainty. However, when the supervisor was on* *vacation or away on business, everyone showed up to work happier and more relaxed."* –Interviewee, college manager

Was this leader aware of their impact on the staff's energy? It's unlikely they intended to have the effect of "I'll show up every day and make sure everyone is fearful and stressed out." Some tweaks to their *presence* could lead to needed improvements.

Think of leadership presence in terms of three areas: *Style, Character, and Substance.* The graphic below is based on the Bates Model of Executive Presence.[25]

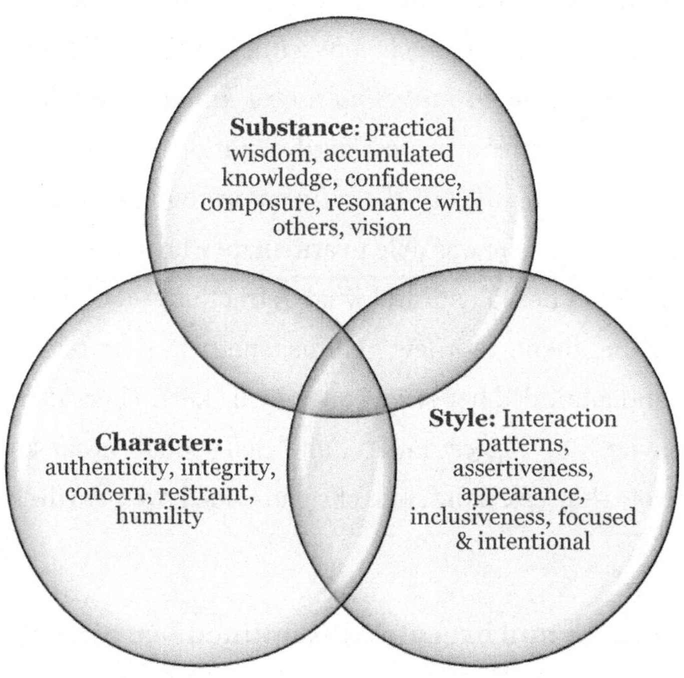

[25] www.bates-communications.com

Reflection: On the previous graphic, circle the themes (from the three areas) where you are already strong. Note areas where you'd like to improve. Include these when you develop a learning plan at the close of this chapter.

The leadership presence elements meld nicely with both the E.Q. and behavioral style attributes addressed earlier. All of them can help you become a highly skilled *people leader*.

One female client, who after reviewing a detailed executive presence (EP) model, took my suggestion to write her own definition of EP. She wrote: *"A way of presenting and being perceived that is grounded in a baseline of self-confidence and experience. It's about matching who I know I am with how others perceive me in professional situations. It's not simply about wearing a suit but there are more complex nuances."* With this clarity, she was able to articulate who she is, what she conveys about her talents and what detractors stood in the way of matching them. In a few months, she better expressed her views and amplified her strong analytical skills. Thereafter, she was invited to bigger tables, and felt equal because she effectively showcased the skills she had honed over two decades.

6. Engage and execute a disciplined learning plan

The best leaders are learners. The well-worn phrase *lifelong learner* is nothing to take lightly when it comes to leaders operating in today's rapidly changing business environment. The best leaders realize the ramifications their leadership has on the business and people; so, they prioritize making time to keep honing their skills, i.e., remaining in a *growth* mode.

This chapter has offered several growth-promoting tools and strategies. What makes them useful is intentionality about building and executing a learning and *unlearning* plan. Tools to improve your competence are varied and accessible.

Think about these **four levels of competence** as you plan.

***1* Unconsciously Incompetent:** This first level is when we are *not aware of* areas where we are unskilled but need to be (blind spots). These are not painful to us, only because we don't yet know about them.

2 Consciously Incompetent: We become aware that we are not skilled through feedback or through self-realization. This level is often unsettling.

3 Consciously Competent: We reach this level through problem-solving, commitment and action; this too is a bit unsettling because here we still need to *consciously* practice with strict adherence to processes and rules; we have not practiced enough to adapt or be flexible; we are not yet masterful.

4 Unconsciously Competent: We reach this mastery level through practice and years of reinforcement. At this level, specific skills or attributes are integrated into our normal behavior without thinking about it.

Note: We continuously move in and out of levels 1-4 as our environment changes, requiring new skills. Expertise is not static; it requires ongoing development to maintain it.

Now, consider these questions:

☑ What are you reading this month? This year?

☑ How are you engaging your talents in new ways to take your team to the next level? (your unconscious competencies)

☑ What *conscious* competencies do you want to develop to move your skills beyond average this year?

☑ What new skills do you need to build? (unconscious and conscious incompetence)

☑ Where should your learning journey begin?

Leader Learning Plan Worksheet

Only 10% of leaders have a learning plan, and most people lack 20-40% of the skills needed to perform their jobs. [26]

On the form, indicate 1) your most value-producing areas for growth (up to three), 2) the expected impact of this growth, 3) the actions (and timeline) you will take to grow in each area.

Growth area examples: *focus on my strengths at work, better listening, better meet direct reports' needs, clarify my vision,* a specific job skill or anything else gleaned from your insights.

Consider a range of activities to help you achieve your goals (*e.g., readings, mentoring, coaching, site visits, coursework, job rotation, certifications, special projects, webinars, conferences, memberships, leadership circles, etc.*).

---

26 Zenger Folkman, Bringing Science to the Art of Coaching, 2014 and Ulrik Christensen, HBR, 9/29/2017

Leader Learning Plan

1. **Growth Area** (Skill or competency)	
Expected Impact	
Development Actions (e.g., readings, courses, projects, visits, mentors, etc.)	**1.**
	2.
	3.
I will complete these actions by (date)...	
2. **Growth Area** (Skill or competency)	
Expected Impact	
Development Actions (e.g., readings, courses, projects, visits, mentors, etc.)	**1.**
	2.
	3.
I will complete these actions by (date)...	
3. **Growth Area** (Skill or competency)	
Expected Impact	
Development Actions (e.g., readings, courses, projects, visits, mentors, etc.)	**1.**
	2.
	3.
I will complete these actions by (date)...	

This is your first draft. Be flexible. As you read further, you may adjust the plan if different skill-building takes precedence.

Here are four examples from four different client I've worked with. These were beginning tasks and based on their individual needs and goals.

Goal	Actions
Build better relationships with direct reports	• Schedule regular one-on-one meetings for updates and to learn about them • Talk less, listen more • Ask for their ideas and feedback
Spend more time being strategic than tactical	• Determine what work is not suitable for my level in the org • Restructure my time to have quiet strategic thinking/planning time blocks
Motivate staff for better performance	• Review performance goals with each person; gather their views on what they need to do their best work • Hold regular check in meetings
Improve delegation to stop doing others' work	• Decide what should be delegated & to who • Read about and apply good delegation • Prepare and inspire people to do the assigned task,clarify expectations, support, check in, debrief, recognize success

Accountability is key to growth. So dedicate specific, realistic chunks of time to establish timelines to complete the actions and determine who you might use as an accountability partner. (Not everyone needs a partner, while some see checking in with a partner as a huge advantage for staying on course.)

After you execute your first plan, celebrate success, then identify more learning goals to continue unleashing your unlimited potential to achieve ongoing masterful leadership.

Fundamentally...*"Leadership is about making others better as a result of your presence and making sure that impact lasts in your absence."*—Sheryl Sandberg

---

This closes Chapter 8, which offered ways to Grow Yourself, recognizing as you grow, so grows your team.

A single leader's greatness, intellect, and energy can only go so far. Building and leading a group devoted to the same vision and goals is key to achieving results beyond one's individual capacity.

Chapter 09
Building a Synergistic, High Achievement Team

If asked about the most salient skills for leading others, I'd say the ability to build a synergized, high achieving team would be at or near the top of the list. This not-so-common competency offers advantages for you, the organization and your direct reports. Among them are *having everyone moving towards the same goals; exchanging ideas and information that enables learning for everyone; each person recognizes and feels valued for their role; members thrive in an environment that exudes equity, purposefulness, collaboration, and support; shared decision-making; accountability for all; and reports of high satisfaction and engagement.*

Concisely, Stephen Covey, says synergy is: *The combined effect of individuals in collaboration that exceeds the sum of their individual effects.*

Based on the 67 interviews for *The Everyday Leader* book (summarized in Chapter 1), these needed attributes for top team performance are in short order.

> *"The least effective managers are prone to open displays of favoritism which undermines the spirit of team. They are reliant on their unconscious biases when making people-related decisions and speaking about their team to others."*
> M. Clark, Millennial HR professional

Skills to build effective teams can be acquired with effort. However, without practice and processes, what will emerge is the opposite of synergistic teamwork. As Patrick Lencioni outlines in his popular *Five Dysfunctions of a Team*, the toxic team environment hallmarks are: 1) distrust (an unwillingness to be open and honest), 2) fear of conflict (avoiding confronting important issues), 3) minimal commitment (to common goals), 4) evading accountability (for self and teammates), and 5) inattention to collective results.

Chapter 9 offers ideas and strategies to improve your adeptness at establishing the conditions for building high-performing teams. The topics are: 1) Review the definition, stages and types of teams, 2) attributes of a high achieving synergistic team, 3) strategies for team development, and 4) designing a work environment for high performance.

1. Review the basics: Definition, stages and types

What is a Team? There is a lot written that is intent on delineating the differences between a work group, individual contributor, and team. Yet, when team is defined *as a group of people that work together towards a common goal and holds each other accountable for achieving that goal*, that's a team concept that fits every leader who has direct reports. This may or may not necessarily apply to short term teams (such as task forces, project teams or affinity groups). For this conversation, it is about you purposefully molding your direct reports into a synergistic group since all of their roles are essential and converge to achieve the goals.

Whether your direct reports are co-located, hybrid or geographically dispersed, the team development approaches that follow will have some application. Virtual work teams have unique nuances, though they are not fully addressed in this chapter. An expanding collection of easily accessible resources exist for those increasingly common scenarios.

Four situations come to mind that make attending to team development a primary focus: 1) when you inherit an existing team, 2) when organizational goals shift dramatically and there's an accompanying need to reshape the team culture and norms, 3) when creating a new team within an organization or department, or 4) when it's necessary for you to rehabilitate or regenerate a dysfunctional set of direct reports.

Why bother? Leaving your direct reports to work in silos can have poor consequences. Assuming each direct report's job role provides an input into your department's goals, if done at a low-quality level, it impacts your and their success.

The team's vital functions: Building and sustaining a high-performing, synergized team is critical to success. As the team's leader, remain attentive to these three critical measures team effectiveness[27].

1. The quality and quantity of the team's work products (the team's *what* and reason the team exists).

2. The team's capabilities—their individual and collective skills applied to achieve their goals (the team's *how* of getting the work done).

3. The team members' demonstrated engagement level, positive feelings and connections to the team—all necessary to achieve at high levels (the team members' *spirit* or *temperament* as they carry out their work, impacting the quality of results and how well they apply their skills).

Consider these cases: Assume you need to achieve aggressive, measurable results within six months to meet your obligations to stakeholders. Yet, three direct reports are doing their job at half-quality and four are intensifying their efforts to help reach

[27] Peters, J. and Carr, C. *High performance team coaching*. 2013.

the goals. An adverse effect on both the results and the team members can be expected. Take another example: Your company says it values customer-centric, best in class service, yet has a few phone-based service representatives who are poor listeners, defensive, and argumentative. Predictably, you receive poor feedback and uneven customer service ratings that run counter to the company's value declarations. And the team falls short of its 90% excellence rating goal.

Building a team helps people get the message that their 1) job roles are important to the organization's success and 2) performance enables the team to meet its goals. Helping to shape and spread healthy attitudes and values across all teammates is critical to high achievement.

Team development is ongoing. When the goals, the leader or any member changes, the culture will lose a bit of its gel. People will again need to know what to expect, what matters most, how their role is affected, and how they will work together.

Stages of Team Development. Bruce Tucker developed the classic four-stage model in 1965. (A fifth stage, Adjourn was added in 1977, but this is not the concern here, for long-term teams.) While it is more than 50 years old, there may still be an opportunity to apply it to your workgroup. Any modification to the team's composition is reason to reconsider what these stages are and what needs to be recalibrated to return to or enhance work at the high-performance stage. So, though simply stated, it takes effort to move to Performing.

Brief Descriptions:

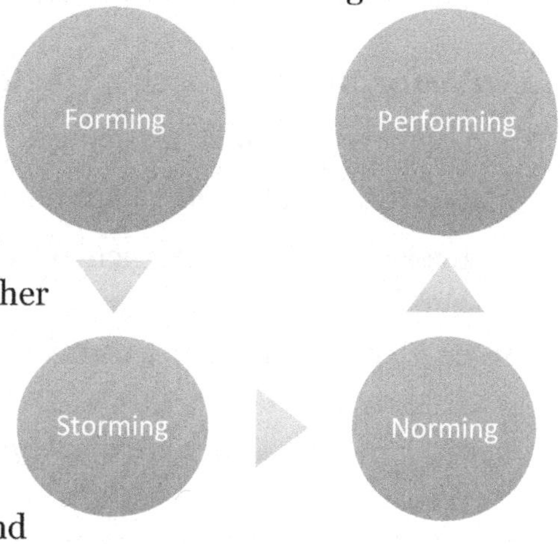

Forming

Performing

Storming

Norming

1. **Forming**. In this first stage, individuals are just coming together and trying to get to know each other. They begin learning each other's stories and styles, their specific roles, meeting schedules, etc.

2. **Storming**. This is the most challenging stage since team members now know each other better. Styles begin to clash, and interpersonal conflicts and challenges to the leader and each other emerge. The leader helps the team members manage the frictions and re-focuses everyone on the goals. Avoidance will trap the team in this stage and inadvertently install a culture of dysfunction.

3. **Norming**. After team members have explored and learned to negotiate their conflicts, the team begins to develop and a healthier culture should have begun taking root. Team members begin appreciating their differences and working together. The leader facilitates norming by chartering the team, encouraging engagement, centering everyone on

shared goals, celebrating successes, and creating a sense of community within a satisfying work environment.

4. **Performing.** At this stage, the team is fully functional, and members are able to manage their relationships, work toward shared goals, communicate openly, experience a sense of belonging and achieve results.

Three Types of Lower Functioning Teams

Type	***Characterized by...***
War Zones	Rivalry, competition, factions, parking lot meetings, loss of attention to larger purpose
Love Fest	Focusing on getting along, avoiding tough issues, insularity (us over them), failure to hold each other accountable, loyalty at all costs ("we are family")
Non-team	Every person functioning separately ("doing my job"), focus on connection to leader, top down, little connection to larger purpose

Ideally, neither of these three team types (there are other ways they are characterized by organizations addressing team development) are descriptive of the state of your team. But don't be surprised if one sounds exactly or similar to your group of reports. That's more reason to act to shift from the typical, fractured team state to a better one. You can begin by looking at the following attributes of high-functioning work teams.

2. Attributes of a high achieving, synergistic team

What does a high achieving synergized team look like? What are the characteristics? Begin by reading the example below.

"My most rewarding experience leading direct reports was the synergy and collaboration that occurred during our design work and projects. The quality of the work was stellar. We often found ourselves in the 'zone' getting the work done. I created a space where the targets and vision were clear. Each of the nine people was encouraged to bring their best thinking, skill, and creativity to the table. We had a non-judgmental feedback process that assisted the team members in developing their capacity. Our unit became one of the top programs in our department due to our collaborative nature."
–educational leadership coach

While there is not a one-size-fits-all set of attributes to describe high performing teams, there are common features that characterize such teams. They are compiled on the next page. Some or all may be useful to your work. Try the next activity to see how well your team is situated.

Assessment Activity: *What's already present in your team's culture of performance?* Use the 20 characteristics below as a checklist (Take it a step further by asking team members to do the same. Then share themes, honor what's working, and choose a few areas for development).

1. ☐ **Clear and shared vision** is articulated, one that emotionally connects team to their roles, goals, and the organization.

2. ☐ **Divergent perspectives** are encouraged and valued, to unleash creativity and engage the intellectual assets of each member.

3. ☐ **Service-oriented leadership**—the leader uses their role to remove barriers and support team's growth in achievement of shared goals.

4. ☐ **Diverse team composition** reflects complementary and varied styles and expertise to achieve goals.

5. ☐ A **team-defined way of working** that clarifies behavioral and communication norms, and how to address conflict and challenges. This team charter is used regularly to guide the desired culture.

6. ☐ **Achieving shared results** is a key focus including measurable, timebound deadlines.

7. ☐ **Supportive structures and processes** are in place for team members to do their work.

8. ☐ A keen sense of **interdependence and trust** to enable sharing practices, thinking and feelings

9. ☐ **Culture of learning** to build more expertise and excellence, never resting on current knowledge

10. ☐ A sense of **emotional safety** wherein team members share feelings, thoughts, and vulnerabilities

11. ☐ **Roles and responsibilities** are **clear** and how they interact and enable all to achieve shared goals.

12. ☐ **High satisfaction** including friendship and fun

13. ☐ Individual and team **performance goals** known to all

14. ☐ **Culture of accountability** is understood and embraced by all in pursuit of achieving shared goals.

15. ☐ **Effective communication** keeps everyone abreast of plans and progress, and there are formal and informal means for storytelling and sharing the right information.

16. ☐ **Stretching beyond the ordinary**—members take on new risks, experience new growth, and increase thriving during adversity.

17. ☐ **Decentralized, shared leadership** is used to build the competencies of team members, to put the best expertise up front when needed.

18. ☐ **Celebrates success**, both small and large, lifting up team members along the way

19. ☐ **High participation** in which members make sure everyone is involved, each voice is valued and never drowned out by other members.

20. ☐ **Planning and preparation** with effective, inclusive mechanisms, processes, input and feedback

Checkpoint: Which 3 to 4 of these might be your top priorities in your initial work to develop your team?

____

____

____

3. Strategies for team development

What follows are four strategies for developing your team: 1) ready yourself as a team builder, 2) team composition, 3) chartering, and 4) better meetings.

Strategy 1: Ready yourself to be a team builder

Here are six simple, difference-making considerations as you do the work to build an effective, synergized team.

1) Review your *Know Yourself* insights (Chapters 6 and 7), your motivations, and beliefs. Then determine how to bring your best to building a talented team; for example, if you have a pattern of poor listening, or insistence on having your way, create reminders to keep these at bay.

Case Story. Clients have asked for team building when what was most needed was cultivating the emotional intelligence of the leader. One nonprofit client shared that her team members were rude, engaged in name calling, unable to make decisions, and untrusting. As the work unfolded, it was clear that the leader—aggressive, demanding, constantly talking over others, and displaying her knowledge of everything conceivable—was setting the tone for their inability to negotiate, reach consensus, try out others' ideas and collaborate. I ended the project, instead suggested leader-coaching as the first step.

2) Build a team around objectives that enhance commitment to the organization and its values; guard against building a cult of personality and loyalty to you.

3) Focus the efforts around achieving some or all of the 20 attributes of high-performing teams described in the previous pages. Advocate for and protect the team from

higher level interference, build capacity and career paths for all, clarify goals, roles, processes and norms.

4) Lead with positivity about what can be accomplished and find ways to engage each team member's strengths.

5) Be consistent and persistent. Don't expect everyone to become warm, trusting and productive overnight.

6) Connect team members to each other. Help answer: *Who's on the team? What's their story? What's each person's job, strengths and valued contributions to the shared goals? How do we best work together?* This could be done during monthly meetings or periodic off-sites. Seek activities that foster mature team relations.

Strategy 2: Team composition

Some leaders inherit their direct reports, and others have a chance to hire part or all of their team. Thinking through team composition is essential work for the leader to achieve their business goals. Here are some basic points that may assist you with assembling a group of people with the potential to be a high-performing, synergistic team.

Put simply: *"Understand the skillset you need for the work and the culture and find people to fit those roles, despite their styles differing from yours."* Interviewee, SVP, national nonprofit

- **Team size** affects the leader's ability to build a synergistic team. When it exceeds 10, it is believed that it becomes too unwieldy to devote the time and resources each person needs to be highly effective.

- **Assess the team make up** in terms of range and diversity of skills, attributes, age and gender, patterns of thinking, styles of communicating and more. Balance the team, for example, with skilled implementers, perhaps introverted, who may be overshadowed by talkative extroverts, who generate ideas yet have difficulty executing.

- **Differentiate, don't clone.** Avoid creating a team with everyone possessing the same skills and attributes as you do. I've heard a leader say explicitly, "I wish I could clone myself," and some build their teams as if this flawed approach is ideal. Assembling a complementary set of styles and skills frees you and your reports to focus on what you and they are best at. Be cautioned, however, that making this work goes beyond just throwing one of these, two of those, etc. into the mix. Attend to the team building principles to experience the benefits of the team's diversity, circumventing team chaos and unending conflict.

Activity: Think about what you need on your team to enable high performance and fulfilling team synergy.

Category	Present on team	Needed on team
Job skills		
Interpersonal attributes		
Types of diverse attributes needed (related to the work)		
Other:		

- **Watch your biases** as you build a team of diverse and relevant skill sets and qualities to enable the team to expand its thinking and move into the future. Unwittingly, our perceptions about people are colored by our preferences for and attractions to certain people traits. This, I've witnessed, is one way the term team or organizational *fit* becomes the culprit for something else; it can let you off the hook for being blinded to the impact of your style and biases on others.

- **Consider human dynamics and core values** when building a team. While work teams should reflect various dimensions of diversity, there are some characteristics all should hold in common to get the work done. Examples in some settings might be collaborative, results-oriented, respect for others' views, etc. So, consider: *How might people synergize with others on the team? What work do I need to do to ensure the team gradually fuses while not losing the potency of each person's unique self?*

- **Attend to the team's conflict management skills.** Any group attempting to work together will inevitably have conflicts among them, since their styles, thinking, and skills are different. This requires you to work with the team to build their collaborative and conflict skills to achieve better synergies. Periodic skill-building sessions might focus on *behavioral styles, emotional intelligence, embracing new perspectives, active listening, empathy and problem-solving processes*. Don't take these for granted.

- **Use a team charter to support decision-making.** Include the team charter elements (later in this chapter) when making decisions about adding new members to your team of direct reports. Any new member will need to come into positive alignment with the charter's agreements.

- **Be decisive when it's time to let go.** On those rare occasions when it's necessary to release team members, think through the potential human and organizational impact along with the best process. Since your expertise may not be HR law and policy, consult with such specialists about the process to avoid a messier transition than necessary. (See *Chapter 14, The Perform Key* for some guidance on sparingly, yet humanely letting go of staff.)

Strategy 3: Develop a team charter

Chartering a team can be transformational. *A team charter is a simple document or roadmap that defines the team's mutual purpose, goals, and how to best work together (norms).* Developing the charter brings together the thinking and strengths of all team members. The process allows the team to move any whispered complaints into meaningful conversations and actions about the team culture and operating environment. Once complete, it is a powerful tool for getting everyone *to row in the same direction* without losing their individual creativity.

A charter becomes a yardstick to hold team members accountable and to bring the team back into alignment if it gradually strays from the charter's tenets. Charters should be reviewed at least annually to determine how well the team is meeting its own expectations and to determine if changes are needed when goals and priorities necessitate adjustments.

Charters should be developed early in the relationship of the leader and their direct reports. Without deliberate clarity, free-developing team patterns will emerge. If you ignore the formation of team attitudes and habits, expect some unfavorable outcomes for the culture and performance. Once poor norms congeal, they are difficult to redirect; shifting the culture is possible, though often requiring losing members.

Charters are developed in one or more team sessions. This fosters buy-in and valuing team members' voices and thoughts. These chartering session(s) are facilitated team conversations around several questions. To improve member's openness to express their thoughts and to evade *groupthink*, use a pre-session survey. Then summarize it for the group to process together in a session.

There are customary items for charters, and many customize them depending on you and your direct reports' priorities, goals, and needed changes to norms. Chartering seeks clarity and agreement on the team's 1) vision, purpose and goals, 2) agreements that govern how the team works together, 3) communication practices, 4) boundaries, 5) process to resolve conflicts and challenges, 6) decision-making authority and process, and 7) expectations for meeting structure and quality.

Sample set of team chartering questions: Below is a sample set of questions developed and used by a team I worked with. Your team can gather questions they believe are equally pertinent to create your desired team culture and standards.

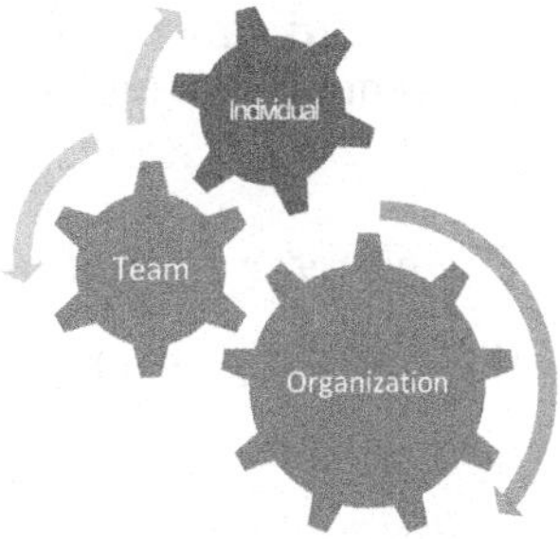

Sample Charter Worksheet

Your vision of who we are to the team and organization: Describe briefly what you would like this to be.____________________________

____

What we deliver: What value do you hope we deliver for the organization?

____

____

How we work together: How can we support each other in taking our next steps? ____________________________________

____

What 3-5 things need to happen to be sure **our meetings** and gatherings are productive, meaningful and satisfying?____________

____

What **has to die** before we can move to something new? ________

____

How should we **meet challenges**?___________________________

____

What would happen that would enable you to feel **fully energized and engaged**? _______________________________________

____

What **pressing needs** require our attention going forward (next 12 months)? ____
____

What's the **next level of thinking** we need to do? ____________
____

What are the team's **capacities and strengths** that we should use more fully? ____
____

What **seed can we plant** today that could make the most positive difference to the future of our work? ______________________
____

The charter should be kept alive. You might keep it posted in the meeting room, place it on agendas, or hand it out occasionally for reinforcement. Revisit it annually to help start a new year of work. Encourage the team to revise the charter if old norms are no longer useful; replace them with better ones.

Strategy 4: Lead more purposeful team meetings

46% of employees rarely or never leave a meeting knowing what they're supposed to do next.[28]

Meetings appear to be here to stay, and lots of them, whether in-person or virtual. Meetings are settings wherein much productive work and team development can take place, but typically don't. Publications abound with guidance for better meetings, masterful meetings, and secrets to great meetings.

---

[28] Gallup.com. State of American Workplace, 2014.

To score a win, bring to life some of the better practices to **make meetings places to strengthen team bonds and produce better results. Meetings can be fruitful, creative, connective, and growth promoting.** Your team will appreciate your effort to make the meetings worthwhile.

Below are a few tips; more are in *Chapter 13 The Develop Key*:

- Meetings should support work, not whittle away work time.

- Have a clear purpose for each meeting. Refrain from distributing agendas with a list of things, but no unifying purpose. Think: *WHY are we meeting? What work do we want this meeting to accomplish? What do I need the team to think through?* If those can't be answered, ask yourself: *Do we need a meeting*?

- Share roles with team members related to *planning* and *leading* the meetings. This builds team efficacy. It works best when the leader provides everyone with specific guardrails so the meeting purpose maintains its focus. This enables those sharing leadership to be creative in their roles while staying true to the meeting purpose and objectives.

- Keep the meetings time efficient and limit the number of items on your agenda so you are able to focus and accomplish what you set out to achieve.

- Provide and try to stick to timeframes for agenda topics so all items are covered. If some items need to go over the time allocated, agree to reschedule topics for future meetings.

- Designate a portion of each meeting to building bonds, learning, generative thinking, and celebration. Some meetings may earmark more or less time for these items.

- Ensure continuity. Connect previous meetings to the next so the team can see they are moving towards some specific objectives. At the start of each meeting, provide time for reporting on previously assigned actions.

- Summarize team decisions and next steps at the close of meetings. Clarify the decisions made, items for future meetings, and assign tasks, responsibilities and due dates.

Activity: For your next meeting, what is one idea to address the following *better meeting* items?

a. **Enhance bonds/connections**

b. **Team share thinking about a work topic**

c. **Celebrate** (what, who)

d. **Learn** (build work or life skills)

e. **Suggestions to plan better meetings**

4. Design the best performance environment

Since one of your primary roles is to ensure your direct reports are inspired, engaged, developing and accomplishing desired results, attend to optimizing the team's work environment. These environment factors were the central theme of Chapter 4, so refer to that chapter again as needed.

Remember your job is to remove barriers and create the best pathway for everyone to do their jobs at a high level. Call to mind, for example, the hallway to get to your workstation. Imagine it is filled with boxes, shards of glass, papers, marbles and more. The simple task of getting off the elevator and walking directly to your desk (or whatever path to your home office) is more complicated than it should be, consumes time, and it becomes frustrating to repeat this maze every day. So, reflect on all of the ways you can remove barriers to your team's performance. Replace them with performance enablers if you want to see them soar.

Pay attention to these essential work environment factors and, in an ongoing way, spend time fine-tuning them:

- Is everyone clear on the goals, roles, expectations?
- Is there provision for effective leader (even peer) coaching, feedback and reinforcement and at the right frequency?
- Does everyone have the tools, processes, resources, and appropriate space to do their jobs well?

- Are there the right and inspiring incentives for desired performance, reinforcements for expected performance, and consequences for less-than-optimal performance?
- Are direct reports provided and encouraged to grow, learn and develop competencies to achieve at higher levels?
- Are all the aspects of and opportunities within the workplace fair and equitable for everyone?

This closes *Chapter 9, Building a Synergistic, High-Achievement Team*. Apply the recommendations that best suit your efforts to build the most effective, high-performance, highly-satisfied, synergized team of direct reports. The benefits are worth it and engaging the talents of a group of people will make your job more fulfilling and with commendable results.

This also concludes **Part Two: Know and Grow Yourself**. The next section specifically emphasizes Knowing and Growing Your People, your #1 job in pursuit of performance excellence.

Part Three

Know and Grow Your People: Five Keys to Help You

The most essential work of the accomplished *Everyday Leader* is to create a team of high-accomplishment direct reports. This requires intention, skill and consistency.

On to Part Three. By now, you've discovered and have begun making progress on some growth areas from your exploration of *Part Two: Know and Grow Yourself.* This section builds on that. The payoff of increasing your self-efficacy will show up as increased mastery leading others and in your overall life. Part Three, *Know and Grow Your People* expands on aspects of the Performance Environment Factors (Chapter 4) by organizing them into Five Keys for becoming masterful people-leaders.

These five chapters can support you in knowing and growing ALL of your people. Actualizing the growth of all of your people, evidenced by their achieving higher levels of accomplishment, is a great indicator of leadership skillfulness.

Too often, lower performing staff receive an inordinate amount of a leader's attention; this is not a good practice. A pattern of punitive actions and scapegoating targeted at these few often sets in. Unsurprisingly, change does not manifest, to the distress of both the leader and the employee. On the other hand, the leader's inattention to average and high performers can lead to their stagnation or unwanted departure. In this scenario, the leader fails to grow as a people-leader, while squandering time on unproductive activities.

These chapters offer you specific areas of competency-building as you lead your direct reports. These five keys can unlock doors for you. They are not a linear process because the keys interact and overlap. Neither are they all-encompassing; but get these indispensable concepts right, and you will experience greater success and happiness leading your team.

Five Keys for Masterful Managers

This section has five chapters:

10. The LEAD Key

11. The CONNECT Key

12. The COACH Key

13. The DEVELOP Key

14. The PERFORM Key

Leadership is all about people...motivating people to get the job done. You have to be people-centered- Colin Powell

Chapter 10

The LEAD Key

Though it may seem obvious that a leader is tasked to *lead*, it is still included as one of the Five Keys covered as essential for effectiveness in your role. I recall a top social sector leader (and coaching client) who believed it was important for everyone to view him as a part of the team. This was well and good, except that this positioning appeared to take precedence over actually leading the team. Yes, the direct reports valued their new leader's ability to collaborate, sincerely garner their input, be accessible, and care about their lives. Yet, in a short time, frustration crept in as they longed for and needed leadership. They yearned for more decisiveness and clarity of vision, values and voice—skills that differentiated him as a leader from a task-list driven, friendly worker bee.

During our coaching partnership, the leader directed his learning towards delineating and exhibiting situationally-appropriate leadership qualities. He targeted strategic and inspirational leadership, finding and expressing his voice, discovering the right balance between consensus and decision-making, honing leadership presence, and developing staff (not just cheering them on). This laser-focus on leading with these aspects present, elevated his leadership, which was met with remarks about him being highly-respected and credible at the top of this high-performance organization.

This chapter speaks to some of those and other characteristics that help people lead well. Topics include: 1) Making the shift and the time to lead others; 2) aligning and inspiring the team with vision and strategy; 3) leading and interpreting systems and culture change; 4) clarifying beliefs, priorities, and non-negotiables; 5) re-thinking leader competence and 6) communicating adeptly across all Five Keys.

High-competence leaders carry out their work from the perspective of the organization's goals. They interpret, align, inspire, and guide the team's work in light of the organization's objectives. They support and manage change, as needed, depending on the organization's evolving priorities. They ensure all team efforts contribute to the larger organizational goals. Alignment requires coordination and collaboration regardless of your leadership level.

Try this: What are your responses to these LEAD questions? Write Yes or No in the box to the right of each question.

1. *Does the leader know the goals?*	
2. *Can the leader identify the value of each direct report's role to the organization?*	
3. *Does the leader work with each team member to develop performance goals and clarify their connection to the organization's goals?*	
4. *Does the leader inspire their team to perform based on the organization and team vision?*	
5. *Does the leader use their voice to raise issues that matter to the organization's success?*	
6. *Does the leader proactively advocate for the needs of the team to remove barriers to them performing well?*	

1. Making the shift and time to lead your people

As the leader, your job is to help people deliver their best at work, which requires dedicating time and establishing the mindset to do that. Maybe you've already made the shift from being a high-performing individual to, as Colin Powell's quote shares, "motivating people to get the job done." As a reminder, I've devised the chart on the next page which illuminates some of the differences between individual achievement and leading an entire group to achieve. **There's a big distinction between leading oneself and leading a group of people to high achievement with ongoing motivation.**

Be sure you are making the shift to the right side of this chart. Individual greatness is no longer the measure of your success.

FROM INDIVIDUAL CONTRIBUTOR...	...TO LEADER OF A TEAM
WORK VALUES: making a personal contribution to the organization; meeting professional standards; integrating into the culture	...ensuring *others* are productive, competent, and motivated; setting direction for and making an impact through *others*; seeing *others* succeed; creating the desired team culture
USE OF TIME: planning own work, improving own work standards; solving everyday problems; focus on "how" to get your work done	...making time for others; getting work done through others; removing barriers for others; divesting self of some individual tasks; focus on "what" we do and "why"
MAJOR SKILLSET: demonstrating expert job knowledge; delivering own tasks on time and with quality	... motivating and coaching others; aligning work with mission; delegating work to others; measuring work of others

Make time: To be effective in maximizing the performance and satisfaction of your direct reports means dedicating time to each one. More often than you'd think, leaders do not meet with their direct reports consistently nor do they *plan* to lead them well. Set a cadence of planned, dedicated time for each person, supported by the belief that this activity is a worthwhile investment. Studies report the ideal amount of time and frequency vary, but a private hour per week or bi-weekly goes a long way; this excludes the 10-minute chats that happen spontaneously during regular work life.

2. Aligning and inspiring around vision and strategy

Whether you are the top leader, mid-level leader, or a front-line leader, your job includes either setting or interpreting the vision, strategies and priorities. And, at whatever leadership level, your team benefits from creating its own guiding vision (as in a team charter [see Chapter 9]) that reflects where the team is going, what it values, and how to get there in support of the organization's vision. For example, *our department envisions delivering the best tools and resources to ensure the organization achieves its goals* or *we work and meet challenges together to assure our customers experience the best-of-the-best service ever*, or whatever it might be.

Your job is to be adept at informing and inspiring, then converting the organizational strategies into your direct reports' job responsibilities and required work results. In this way, the organization is better able to achieve its goals.

Each direct report should know and be reminded that their job is a crucial, valued ingredient in the formula for organizational success. They should be keenly aware of the direct connection between their job results and achieving the business's goals. Since each report should know they play a role in fulfilling the strategies and vision of the organization, they should know what the strategies are (the big picture) and personalize it by linking their job to it (a part of making the big picture happen). Regrettably, most don't know the company's goals, thus are content to work in compartmentalized ways, which reduces productivity. Who's partly culpable for this "just doing my job" siloed mindset? You guessed it—the leader makes a difference.

> *"Employees feel frustrated when managers fail to help them connect their role to the bigger picture. The modern workforce wants a job that feels meaningful. They need to be able to see clearly how their role contributes to the success of their team and organization. When employees have this sense of purpose, their engagement soars."* (SOAW, 2017)

Times will arise when your staff's roles and responsibilities may need to be realigned—typical when new strategic priorities are created. People tend to resist changes in their job tasks year-to-year since they have developed good patterns for their work. (Having such patterns enables staff members to build expertise and experience). Yet, job requirements will inevitably change for the good of the organization. The challenge arises when the leader doesn't clarify why some job segments need to change—to sync with the business's new aspirations.

Confirm and Affirm: It's your job to ensure staffers are on board with and inspired by changes the organization's goals require of them. Periodically, refresh and affirm direct reports about the worth of their jobs. Without reinforcing the *why* of each job, tasks can become stale and attitudes can sour.

A strategic focus requires planning time. Masterful leaders organize themselves so they have time and mental space to plan to lead their teams. Others view spending time thinking and planning rather than being 100% hands-on not useful. Yet, preparing for the team to move beyond the daily job demands is a differentiator between a strategic leader and a tactical one.

So, observe how you allocate your time. *Are you devoting enough time to the most important things?* Consider how Stephen Covey[29] delineated time allocation in Quadrant 2. Planning and preparation activities are in that box. Covey also refers to Q2 as the *quality and personal leadership* quadrant or the *Important but Not Urgent* work. Are you carving out time to plan for the future of the team's work? (*See Appendix for a four-quadrant activity to better allocate your time.*)

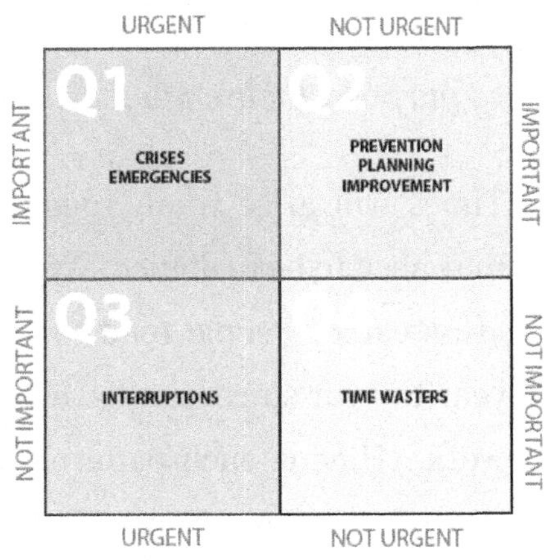

One client began a practice of blocking time for strategic thinking work (60 minutes a week initially). After a few weeks, she reported feeling a greater sense of accomplishment, which boosted her confidence, knowing that she was now functioning at a level more compatible with her job title.

[29] Covey, S. *First Things First*, 1994.

3. Lead and interpret systems and culture change

As a leader, one of your functions is to align processes, systems and the culture as the organization's goals change. And in situations where you become the new leader, and there are entrenched misalignments of work processes and cultural norms, this is a chance to assess then dismantle the old, ineffectual structures. You must, at the same time, begin installing better processes that remove obstructions and open the way to better performance and job satisfaction for your people. Whether you're a newly-hired leader or one that has the task of taking the team through organizational change, leaving processes and cultural norms intact that are no longer useful can have longer-term debilitating consequences.

It's empowering for your direct reports to be included in analyzing the systems and culture. Work with the team to redesign elements in ways that make their and the company goals more achievable. Your strategic insight and the benefits of the changes will go a long way.

Advocate and avoid landmines: Another key aspect of leading your team through systems and culture change is possessing good organizational (political) savviness. This enables you and your team to be change-adaptable and avoid some of the landmines along the way. Far too often, mid-level or even top-level leaders are aggrieved by changes that take place at a level above them. Some are overt in their complaints and resistance, while others whisper in their attempt to undermine the change initiative. They are unwittingly paving the way for their and even their team's demise.

Rather than seeking to understand decisions and serve as an informed, mature advocate to help improve upon the changes, unsophisticated leaders steer the team down the wrong paths. Political savviness means knowing where the levers of control are and who the key influencers are, which can help you discover points of influence and ways to navigate the changes.

I've worked with clients who built their early leadership style around the rightness and fairness of organizational decisions. That's noble, but usually there is little appreciation for the complexities involved in decision-making. At times, mid-level leaders, have only partial information, and they pair that with an egotistical belief that their way is the best and only way.

To be more effective within the ambiguity of organizational politics, recognize first that politics exist in every organization, and can be used for either good or bad. Next, build your political muscle and stamina to prepare you to approach the changes as a better advocate for removing any barriers the changes present related to getting your team's work done. To advocate doesn't mean arguing unceasingly. It means offering alternative suggestions that can be wins for everyone. It means having the capacity to see the world from more than your perspective. Enhanced political stamina fortifies you to move forward once final decisions are made, allowing you to steer your team to embrace and grow with and through the changes.

Reflection: Some considerations as you interpret and lead change (these questions might be useful to help your direct reports adapt to change as well):

- *What systems are helping us achieve our goals and which need to be adjusted?*
- *What processes are no longer as effective as they could be in achieving our goals?*
- *Which of our cultural norms help us live up to our commitments to our stakeholders and each other?*
- *Which cultural norms do we need to do away with because they prevent us from moving into the future successfully?*
- *What can I and the team do to recalibrate our systems, processes, and norms to take our work to the next level in support of the organization's goals?*
- *Are there better ways of achieving goals that deserve my attempts at advocacy?*
- *Is the work effectively distributed to my direct reports, or should alterations be made to better align skills, strengths and job responsibilities?*

4. Clarify beliefs, values, priorities, non-negotiables

Leaders who articulate who they are and their beliefs, values and priorities are perceived as better leaders than those who don't. You probably recall less-respected leaders who preface every statement with "*They said* we have to or need to..." or those who never express convictions about important issues.

A colleague once shared her frustration regarding her company tag line supervisor. "I don't know what this guy believes. He's like a robot with pat answers. He acts powerless over everything, always saying 'the higher ups said we have to do this,' so he allowed for no deviations, not even on little things. I didn't trust him to have our backs on anything."

This leader had not developed their own voice, reflecting an underdeveloped *leader presence.* Masterful leaders interpret goals and decisions through their own words, stories, and beliefs.

What do you believe? What is your point of view as issues arise? What's the basis for your views? How do you express passion for your work? Have you clarified the non-negotiables, so your direct reports know their work and decision boundaries? For example, one nonprofit said, "We don't take funds from gaming or tobacco industries." A school declared, "We don't equivocate about our belief that *all* students can achieve at high levels."

Lead with Presence: As noted in the *leadership presence* section of Chapter 8, attend to matching your *intended* way of being (your *presence*) with your *actual* way of showing up. Misalignment in the two can diminish your credibility among direct reports and colleagues. Recall the three *presence* areas:

- *Character:* Which character traits are most important for how I show up? Do I lead in a way that make my deepest held beliefs, values, and ethics visible?

- *Style:* What are the attributes of my personal style that signal I am a leader? Is it more of a priority for to me to be everybody's friend or to be a mature, skilled and respected professional? Am I tolerant of divisiveness or undermining remarks that diminish staff members, or do I ensure direct reports address their concerns with each other in a productive way?

- *Substance:* Do I bring substance and maturity to how I show up? Is my voice an informed, inclusive one? Am I composed and confident when speaking about weighty matters, supported by knowledge of the issues?

5. Revisit: Model for high-achieving leadership

As you LEAD, pay attention to the general attributes of a high-achieving leader.

Activity: Using the chart below (from Chapter 3), which of these are your areas of great strengths? Now, circle the qualities that are not in your area of great strength yet are important for the work you do currently and will do in the near future. Consider 1-2 for development planning.

Task-Centric "Getting Exceptional Work Done"	People Centric "Creating a Staff Culture for Success"
• Visionary & Strategic	• Emotionally Mature
• Decisive	• Empathetic/Humane
• Good Business Acumen	• Honest and Trusting
• Role-specific Skills	• Connects/Friendly
• Professionalism	• Effective, clear communicator
• Collaborative	• Good Listener/Patient
• Influencing	• Inspiring/ Motivating
• Accountable/Reliable	• Effective Feedback
• Risk taking/ Innovative	• People Developer
• Committed to Mission	• Transparent
• Change adaptable	• Being Fully "Present" with people
• Diplomatic	• Inclusiveness
• Political/Context Savvy	
• Resilience in adversity	

One area often overlooked is identified in the table as *Inclusiveness.* Welcoming and inviting each direct report into the team and demonstrating fairness across the team are imperative. Grievances about favoritism among direct reports are common. As the leader, you are tasked with creating and sustaining an environment in which everyone's talents and perspectives are respected and engaged. With you, support, encouragement and challenge are ever-present, enabling each report to do the best job they can. Ensuring and championing inclusivity and fairness—that's your job.

6. Communicate adeptly across the Five Keys

Every leader owes it to those they are leading to be a skillful communicator. That entails communicating clearly, honestly, humanely, impactfully, and with appropriate discretion. Communication (Latin for "sharing") has a wide-ranging impact, and low-quality communication is cited as one of the major complaints in organizations. Whether you are communicating goals, challenges, decisions, delegating, or providing feedback, your manner, timing, and clarity can make work life easier or cause frustration and confusion, which can deplete everyone's time. **Communication is one of the indispensable competencies for all leaders.** Investing in strengthening your skills in this area will take you far, even further than many technical skills will.

Communication is a *system* for sending and receiving messages. It's a two-way process for reaching mutual understanding, in which participants not only exchange information, ideas and feelings but also create and share meaning. Represented in the graphic on the next page, communication is complex, and objective communication is a fallacy given that *everything we say, hear, write, and express (e.g., through body language) is filtered through our and others' lifetime of experiences and beliefs.* Those create *interference* with message clarity. So, the best leaders work on being increasingly effective in this area.

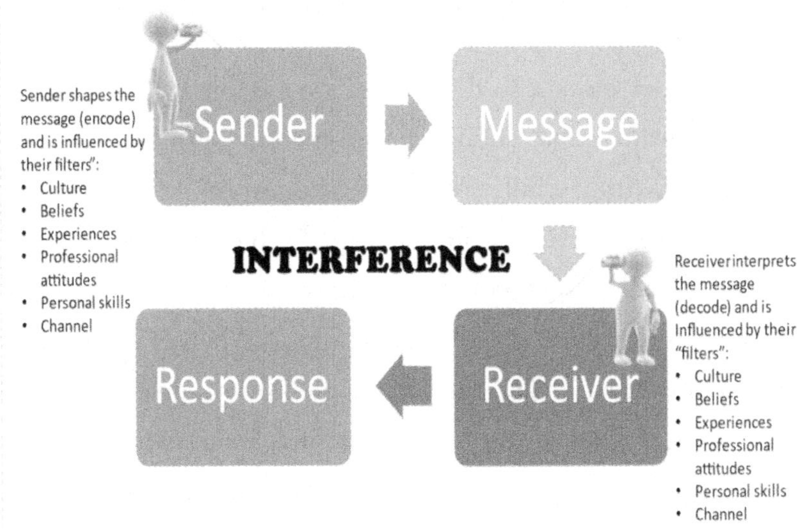

"To effectively communicate, we must realize that we are all different in the way we perceive the world and use this understanding as a guide to our communication with others." -Anthony Robbins

Communication Checkpoint Activity: Think about your communication strengths and challenges, then respond to the two questions below.

1. What three (3) ways do my communication habits help me collaborate, listen, respond and lead my team well?

____

____

____

____

2. What are 1-2 habits that I might address to enhance the quality of my communication?

____

____

____

Review this chart as you consider better practices.

COMMUNICATION Positive Attributes	COMMUNICATION Detractors
• Active listening • Appropriate posture, body language • Eye contact • Clear and concise when speaking • Openness to different points of view • Impulse control; think before you speak • Demeanor of confidence, friendliness, good tone • Empathy and respect • Selection of the best communication channels for different situations	• Unwillingness to listen • Over-communication • Conflicting information • Language and style differences (e.g., gender, regional) • Prejudice (prejudgment) based on diverse characteristics and status • Disinterest • Negative emotions and tone • Filtering (distorting or withholding info) • Selective perception • Ineffective body language • Lack of source credibility

Advocacy and Inquiry: One area that causes leaders to stumble is the tendency, during conversations, to mostly advocate for their own positions and give little time genuinely listening to other perspectives. Several of the 67 interview respondents and clients remarked that their leader doesn't listen, shows an obsessive *need* to be right, imposes their views, or is stubbornly set on their way without ever considering others' thoughts. This describes a leader lacking inquiry skills who over-advocates (and with poor quality).

ADVOCACY is.... stating YOUR view (expressing YOUR opinion, urging action YOU think is important).

High quality advocacy is demonstrated by.... Stating your views well, describing what you think, expressing a judgment with a reasoned rationale, urging a course of action with your reasoning clarified. Avoids dictating.

INQUIRY is.... asking questions (with genuine *curiosity* to understand the thinking or reasoning of OTHERS)

High quality inquiry is demonstrated by...asking high quality questions, facilitating conversations, encouraging dialogue and debate, welcoming input and feedback, and seeking the wisdom in the room. It's earnest and doesn't come across as interrogating.

Advocacy and inquiry are complementary communication behaviors useful for leaders when carried out appropriately. There are leaders who are uncomfortable with advocacy; they tend to shy away from taking a stance on important issues or standing up for the needs of their direct reports.

Examples of high- and low-quality advocacy and inquiry. **Which *of the following sound more like you?***

Low quality advocacy	High quality advocacy
I've got expertise in this, so it is what it is.	Here's what I think and here's how I got here.... Do you see it differently?
Doing it my way makes the most sense.	I came to this conclusion based on... or let me provide a few examples that clarify what I'm proposing...
It just works that way.	*After stating a position:* What do you think about what I just said? Are there any flaws in my reasoning? Or what can you add?
I've pretty much got this down pat, so I'm good.	Here's an aspect that I'd like you to help me think through...
Low quality inquiry	**High quality inquiry**
You get what I'm saying, right?	What are your thoughts about what I'm saying?
This is the best idea, don't you think? You agree, right?	How do you see it? Or how do you view it different from my view?
Why don't you just do this?	What might it take for you to do this effectively?
Why didn't you just say that when it happened?	What made it difficult for you to speak up? Is there something I might do differently the next time to encourage you to speak up?

Strive for both **balance** and **quality** to demonstrate what mature communication looks like for your direct reports.

Lead at a higher level by communicating.....

- ☑ *Clearly*: Accurate, complete, focused, and concise; try paraphrasing to ensure the message sent and how you or the other person received it match. *Paraphrasing* is to restate, in your words, what you believe the person said to confirm clarity before providing your response.

- ☑ *Receptively*: Actively listen to others; be open to hear alternate points of view.

- ☑ *Inclusively*: Encourage, respect and leverage other and varied viewpoints to improve your thinking and acting.

- ☑ *Assertively*: Speak up confidently, directly, honestly, and appropriately; at the same time recognize the emotions and needs of others. (Find the right balance between passive [as if your feelings/thoughts don't matter] and aggressive [as if your feelings/thoughts are the only ones that matter]).

- ☑ *Sufficiently*: Know what needs to be communicated and what doesn't.

- ☑ *Timely*: Do not let problems fester without addressing them; that demoralizes others. Consider the best time to address issues. Find the soonest and best window of opportunity or teachable time.

☑ *Appropriately*: Communicate praise publicly and corrective feedback and personal concerns privately.

☑ *Humanely*: Show regard for the humanity of each person. Address people's actions, not their personhood. Consider your tone, empathy, and language.

Chapters 12 and 13 provide more communication support in their coverage of Coaching, Feedback, and Delegation.

Closing Reflection: This chapter has addressed several topics related to the LEAD key. Review the chapter's themes, then jot down the biggest ideas from this section that you want to dig into a bit more as you LEAD your direct reports.

☑
☑
☑
☑

This closes *Chapter 10, The Lead Key*. The next chapter examines *The Connect Key*, another key behavior for leading direct reports to performance excellence.

Your greatest ability to impact the performance of your team is through your relationship with them, not through your title.
–K. Grant, Senior Executive

Chapter 11

The CONNECT Key

It is often said that people will do more for those they like and respect than for those they don't. We see this when there are good matches between mentor and mentee or teacher and student. Some students report learning to enjoy a subject based on a positive feeling about the teacher, while others came to dislike a subject based on a negative teacher sentiment. At work, when direct reports have a sense of positive relatedness with their supervising leader, the outcomes tend to be better.

> *"Sometimes people attempt to hide behind roles–executive, parent, boss–they have the power or authority of the role replace the relationship. It won't work. Roles may provide the circumstances, but only the relationship can provide the foundation."*[30]

---

30 Flaherty, J. Coaching, *Evoking Excellence in Others*, 3rd Ed, 2010, pg. 47

As the leader, build connections early; it is critical to leading people well. If possible, avoid rushing to fix your direct reports' problems before building quality connections with them. (This wouldn't apply if you are hired as a turn-around specialist with the express purpose of spending six months changing systems, structures and staff before exiting the role.)

Chapter 11 addresses: 1) What does it mean to connect? 2) ways to build connections with direct reports, 3) uncover strengths, talents, and preferences, and 4) steering clear of building poor, biased or compromising connections.

1. What does it mean to Connect?

To connect means leaders, for one, skillfully build relationships with each direct report, genuinely listening and engaging to learn of their strengths, interests, challenges and development needs. Such leaders know and care about each direct report's work *and* life story, since people bring their whole selves to work. Leaders attend to sustaining a relationship of trust, openness, respect and credibility with each direct report.

> *"The relationship between manager and employee represents a vital link in performance management. Managers can be confident that employees do want to interact with them and talk to them about work and life. Gallup research has found that employees are more likely to be engaged when they strongly agree they can approach their managers with any*

type of question and talk with them about non-work-related issues." –State of American Workplace, 2017

Connection Reflection Questions: Ask yourself these questions and if you don't have an answer, take the steps to be able to give specific responses in the near future:

- *What do you do to intentionally build authentic relationships with each of your people?*
- *How well do you practice actively listening?*
- *Is it your habit to gather input from team members about their strengths, preferences, and needs?*
- *Do you encourage your staff to share ideas and truly listen?*
- *In what ways do you lift up or celebrate what's working well?*
- *Do you demonstrate equitable treatment of all direct reports?*
- *Do you show up with authenticity, concern and integrity to encourage your staff to be open with you?*

Connect before you Correct (if possible). Feedback designed to improve performance is more easily accepted and acted upon when staff members have a trusting, respectful relationship with the leader. Quality relationships open the way for a leader to offer difficult feedback with candor—sincerely and directly.

2. Ways to build connections with direct reports

The more you know about your direct reports (and they know about you) as whole humans, the better the sense of relatedness and the greater the loyalty to working to achieve the team's goals. This does not mean to be intrusive or violate their or your boundaries by attempting to delve into people's personal lives.

> *"...these relationships do not follow the rules of other relationships in our lives; they require a careful balancing act. You need to care personally, without getting creepily personal or trying to be a 'popular leader'."*[31]

Connecting doesn't require spending unending time in social, after-work activities; they can be made by such behaviors that ensure authentic connections, including:

- ☑ Making sure each person feels heard; listen intently and ask for input to know what they are thinking
- ☑ Expressing interest and concern by listening to each person's life stories to learn what motivates them
- ☑ Providing specific praise for valued accomplishments, early and often
- ☑ Ensuring each person feels psychologically safe when expressing their views, making mistakes.
- ☑ Asking about career and growth goals to support them in getting where they want to go in the future

[31] Scott, K. Small talk is an overrated way to build relationships with your employees. HBR, June 25, 2017.

- ☑ Being interested in others: *"You will be more successful by being interested in others' success than by trying to get them interested in your success"* (Dale Carnegie).

- ☑ Allowing staffers to set the agenda for meeting with you

- ☑ Seeking feedback on what you can do to be even more effective in supporting them

- ☑ Recalling names of spouses/partners and children; and challenges and celebrations shared with you, etc.

- ☑ Taking the first few minutes of one-on-one meetings to inquire about how things are going for them (before jumping right into business)

- ☑ Beginning team meetings with simple, work-related reflections that encourage staff to share their thoughts and feelings. Sample questions: *What was the best part of your work week? What work made you feel the most gratified or the most frustrated? If you could re-do one of your work tasks, how might you go about it?*

A Connection Story. *"My most rewarding experience with my supervisor was when he saw that I was 'off my game' and he approached me with, 'What's going on? You're not yourself.' And what made it rewarding was he took off his supervisor hat and became 'a human being.' He was empathetic and listened to what was going on. He then said,*

'What can I do to support you?' And then he offered to reduce my responsibilities so I could focus on what I needed to do to get back on track." -Interviewee, HR Executive

3. Discover strengths, talents and preferences

To raise the productivity of your direct reports, be constantly vigilant about learning and recognizing what is *distinctive* about each person and how those differences can add value to the work. To thrive and achieve at work, leaders and our team members should be provided work responsibilities that make use of their strengths and talents most of their time at work.

These unique attributes can help the team do its work better and faster. How much time is wasted trying to find who can help on this or that project? Knowing the strengths of each person makes it easier to direct people to the right resource persons. Such awareness can help you figure out how to best help teammates work together, rather than clash? It also helps you to customize roles and design projects to better engage your team's known and underutilized strengths.

How much do you know about what your team members are able to do and contribute at work?

How can you uncover these gifts and powers? Most managers don't have a process to do so, yet it doesn't have to be difficult. One way is to simply make time to ask. Try questions like: *What aspects of the work bring you the most fulfillment? Which work tasks would you like to spend even more time on? How would you describe your areas of great interest and skill? What are you good at that we probably don't even know about? If you could trade off a few tasks in order to give commitment to others, which would those be?* The last question can help you redirect (or reduce) the least satisfying work to give more time on tasks that are more satisfying and value-adding.

Another way is to use strengths-focused assessments (e.g., Strengths Finders or DISC behavioral styles) that reveal some of the unique attributes of each person. Be sure to spend time processing through them and creating opportunities to better deploy those strengths in service to the goals.

A Story: Unrecognized and under-engaged talents.

How much talent are you leaving on the table? During a facilitated workshop, 30 participants were asked to jot down a list of their strengths, those things they do better than most, that people say they "make look easy", that they can do without regard for time, and that they frequently hear compliments about. Next, they were asked to take each one and indicate which of these strengths they get to use a lot at work and which they rarely or ever use at work.

Then we asked each person to take the strengths from their "rarely used at work" list and write each one on a Post-It note and place it on a tabletop that was set up in the room. These were identified as just a sampling of talents the organization was leaving on the table.

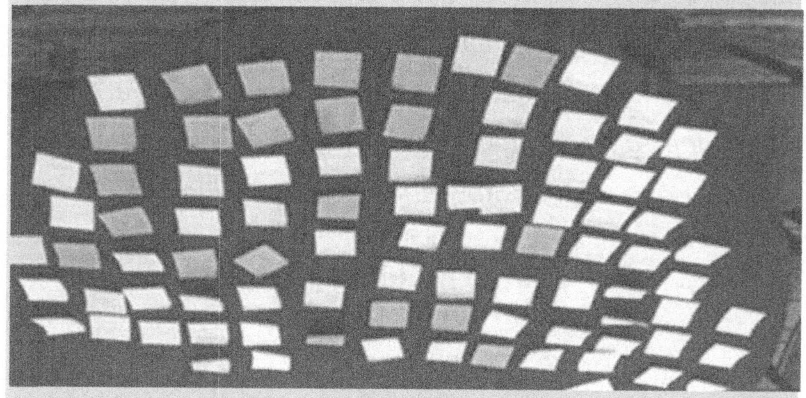

Brains began churning about how some of these strengths could be applied to various work situations, whether they were workplace skills or artistic ones. This revealed the potential to engage so much more of what staffers can contribute to the organization and their work every day.

With enough time and focused attention, strengths can be brought to the forefront, while building connective tissue throughout the team. The next steps then were to create strategies to leverage all this potential for the good of the organization and the staff—a possible win-win situation, since people who get to use their strengths at work perform better.

Uncover Preferences: The other part of connecting well is knowing what kind of interactions and work styles are best for each direct report. Some individuals want to know the big picture and expected job outcomes, then be given the autonomy to design how to carry out the role and be evaluated on the results. Others want step-by-step support. Try questions like this to ask periodically (and individually): *What are your preferences regarding how we work together? How do you want me to support you in doing your best work? What do you hope I don't do as a supervisor? Will you describe what your ideal working relationship with a supervisor looks like?*

4. Steer clear of building poor, biased or compromising connections.

Another consideration for building connections is to attend to possible connection pitfalls, from which it can become difficult to recover. Look at a few of these below:

- *Building boundary-less friendships.* While it's known that having a best friend at work leads to higher staff retention and other advantages, your job is not to make best friends of your direct reports. This can be a delicate balancing act, but much is at stake. Being respected, accessible, and relational are important, and setting boundaries is an essential part of that credibility and perceptions of fairness with and among your direct reports. Oversharing, bad-mouthing others, and breaching confidentiality can become pitfalls difficult to overcome. Set boundaries to maintain a professional, yet cordial, supervisory relationship.

- *Instances where your friend and colleague becomes your direct report.* This can be tricky, so think about how to re-balance the friendship so it remains healthy, collegial, and affable rather than distance yourself and become their authoritative boss. This too diminishes credibility. I recall a client sharing: "When he became my boss, our friendship ended." It was a sign to this client that the leader was insecure in the elevated role and had to prove "I'm now your boss."

- *Guard against sharing either personal or performance information among direct reports.* They will find out. How well you keep confidences is also an indicator of whether people can trust you. Can they? Maintain trust.

- *Watch out for biases in your connections.* Pay attention to whether someone's style, beliefs, traditions, etc. are blinding and biasing you against them despite their ability to perform. Support every direct report in achieving their goals by leading inclusively.

- *Do not freely share your insecurities in your role with those you lead.* At times, there will be people who report to you that perhaps could do your job as well as you can. Yet, they don't have the job, you do. Build your connections around their strengths and how to leverage them not by comparing yourself to them or making remarks that indicate you are uncertain about your ability to do the job. This undermines perceptions of your worthiness for the job, causing staffers to wonder why you're in the role and earning a higher salary than they do. Try to live up to your role, developing yourself so you increasingly do better at it. (See the next item.)

- *Watch for biases against high talent staffers.* Some leaders feel intimidated by high performers or *smart* people. These staffers are sometimes unfairly labeled as difficult—*not team players.* Others are enigmas for leaders who think, "Wow, they are really smart; I'm not sure what to do with them." Recognize their benefit and uncover ways use their unique and complementary expertise to achieve team goals at even higher levels. This frees you for other projects needing your attention.

The high-talent team *plus* factor. I had the privilege to experience first-hand leading leaders with vastly more experience in the business's operations than I had. I assessed their talents by asking questions, reviewing their resumes and work products. From there, I chose my plan and style of leading them. I understood my job was not to do their jobs—for which they had expertise. Instead, my job was to figure out how to best deploy and maximize those skills to achieve better results. I focused on enhancing and directing my leadership towards boosting their confidence and competence to achieve at even higher levels. This was one of my best experiences - leading by freeing people to do what they do best and in better ways.

Apply suggestions from this chapter as you better activate the CONNECT key to leading others. Use the plan below.

Closing Activity: My Connect Plan

Here's an opportunity to give more thought to taking your Connect Key skills up a notch.

Instruction: Using the space below, think about, then list three actions you will take to ensure you adopt practices to build effective relationships with each direct report. Next, identify any direct reports with whom you need to pay more attention to the quality of your connection.

Three practices to enhance Connections with direct reports

(1)

---

(2)

---

(3)

I will pay more attention to the quality of my connection with these specific direct reports: ______________________

This closes *Chapter 11, The Connect Key*. Build relationships in an ongoing way and in coordination with the other of the Five Keys to masterfully lead your direct reports.

To be an effective coach, most managers need to adjust the content of their conversations, as well as their approach to employee communication."[32]

Chapter 12

The COACH Key

Employees today come to work with skills acquired through many channels thanks to advances in technology. They are informed and yearn greater self-direction. Leaders committed to developing the highest performing, innovative and change-adaptable staff teams become proficient *leader-coaches.* The command-and-control bosses cannot create the conditions for their teams to meet the challenges of the modern workplace.

Taking on a *leader-coach* approach means growing new skills. Various studies, and my own observations, reveal that many who say they're coaching, aren't. They are directing, advising, trying therapy, or acting as motivational speakers. There's a place for these, but when it comes to coaching direct reports, know when you're coaching rather than doing the others.

[32] Gallup.com. State of American Workplace, 2017.

Your aim as the coaching-leader is to convert talent into performance.

Before delving into sharpening your coaching skills and applying that approach, be reminded that the relationship (connection) forms the foundation for effectively coaching your people to deliver their best work. Even if leaders perform the right coaching activities with their staff, *"all of these will fail to yield any benefits if the foundation of a solid relationship does not exist."*[33]

Chapter 12 addresses the COACH key using these topics: 1) What coaching can do for you, 2) your readiness for coaching, 3) a coaching framework, 4) from telling and advising to listening and inquiring, and 5) mastering the art of feedback.

1. What coaching can do for you

Let's first take a look at what it means to coach at work. I've developed the view that: *Coaching at work is a series of conversations that enable direct reports to unlock their inner-resources to achieve in their work and personal lives with increasing effectiveness and fulfillment. It is about a leader embracing a style of leading and developing their people that produces new insight, facilitates growth and unleashes the strengths of their reports (which also grows the leader).*

[33] Zenger and Stinnett, *The Extraordinary Coach*, , p. 62.

Note: Workplace coaching differs from coaching with an external coach, especially as it relates to the client's level of vulnerability and exposure. *Remember*: Being coached by one's supervisor is great, but they are still the supervisor who evaluates performance, whereas an external coach is not.

Here are a few more definitions of coaching to ensure a common understanding as you go through this chapter.

"interactions that help the individual being coached to expand awareness, discover better solutions, and make and implement better decisions." (Zenger, p. 44)
"an efficient, high-impact process of dialogue that helps performers improve results in ways that are sustained over time."[34]
partnered, thought-provoking process that inspires people to maximize their personal and professional potential. (International Coaching Federation)

Workplace coaching begins by recognizing you are *applying coaching as an approach* to heightening performance. Supervisors ought to remain cognizant that they have two roles (coach and supervisor) and not conflate the two. Managers "*hold employees accountable for results, while a coach helps people improve the skills needed to achieve those results. [Those managers] who coach both mandate the goals and help people develop the ability to accomplish them.*" [35]

I agree with the personal agency-building that James Flaherty[36] describes as the products of coaching: *long-term*

[34] Neitlich, A. *Coach!*, 2016, p. 13
[35] O'Neill, M., *Executive Coaching with Backbone and Heart*, 2007, p. 262
[36] Flaherty, J. *Coaching, Evoking Excellence in Others*. 3rd Ed, 2010.

excellent performance, self-correction and self-generation. In essence, coaching builds people's own resources to achieve at high levels without endless external input (i.e., supervision).

Benefits for the leader: Building coaching skills will have advantages for you, your direct reports and colleagues (who might model your successful coaching). Coaching skills:

1. create a culture of co-accountability *with* direct reports.
2. lead to lasting transformation with its future focus on achieving better actions, thinking and results.
3. develop your leadership since coaching is two-way, i.e., you provide and seek it through feedback from your direct reports.
4. uncover more possibilities and potential within direct reports (who are rarely asked their thoughts or reasoning).
5. build bonds and loyalty to the organization and the team.
6. express your belief in each person's capacity to think, act, and grow better, differently, and creatively.
7. free your time for higher level work as increasingly capable direct reports apply their talents to more complex tasks.
8. help create a culture of learning and continuous growth.
9. support developing new leaders for organizational succession.
10. make you more flexible in your approach to solving problems.
11. provide a *framework* to help your direct reports grow.
12. bring more interest, quality and inspiration to the meeting time you spend with your direct reports.
13. distribute solution-finding and decision-making, easing pressure on you to have all the answers.

Reflection: Which of the above 13 benefits excite you the most as you make the shift to a coaching leader?

____

____

2. Your readiness and conditions for coaching

Check your beliefs: Coaching is built on the premise that people are resilient and capable of *self-correction* (*recognizing whether they are doing well or not and adjusting their actions to improve*) and *self-generation* (they can independently discover ways to improve). As such, rather than the leader being bossy and directive when something doesn't go well, it's likely the employee already has a good idea about their errors. So, feedback coaching might begin with: *What's your view of the project's outcome? What worked well that you'd do again? What would you have liked to work better? What ideas do you have to approach the issue differently the next time?*

The coaching-leader holds a positive belief about the potential of their direct reports to problem-solve.

Not a quick, simple shift: Later, this chapter will present what appears as a simple framework to move you from always directing, telling and advising to listening and asking; applying the model will require you pay attention to making some shifts. You will probably be surprised when you become aware of how much you give orders (even if nicely) rather than inquiring (often a better tactic). Telling is quick; it comes naturally for many of us, but, in the long run, it restricts growth. So, practice, even if you need sticky note reminders that say *"Listen, don't tell. Wait. Let them think before you jump in."*

The limits of telling and directing: Staff members do not always need the leader's solutions to *their* situations. They need the leader's skills in helping them discover their own solutions and the leader's belief in their ability to do so. Solutions for one person are rarely the same for the next.

Be prepared: Your scheduled one-on-one meetings can be part check-in and part coaching. There is no need for you to label it a coaching meeting; the main thing is to apply a *coaching approach* to address challenges and opportunities. If the meeting is 60 minutes, maybe 10-15 minutes can be spent on updates and the rest on work-related coaching. The direct report should play a key part in choosing the meeting *topics,* while you mostly focus on the meeting *process*. Be flexible.

Prepare your mind and the coaching space. Coaching requires your full attention. That means arranging for a private space and being fully present (without distraction). This allows you to listen intently and ask questions that enable rather than block thinking. A sample set of questions (later in this chapter) might be useful as you transition to a coaching leader style.

Prepare your direct reports: If your style is not already a growth-promoting coaching one, when you make the change, your staff may initially be thrown off. Though you don't need to announce, "I'm coaching you," you might let them know that you are changing to what you believe is a better approach to the one-on-one meetings. Let them know the meetings will be more valuable by 1) focusing more on their growth and development not just updates, 2) spending time hearing what's on their mind and topics of interest to them, 3) helping you learn more about the work from them since they are closer to the work and likely have solutions and insights, and 4) checking in on the usefulness and quality of your one-on-one meetings. (See *Appendix* for a sample coaching format.)

Be mindful of your reason for coaching: You aim to encourage your direct reports to make better choices, increase problem-solving confidence, expand thinking and beliefs to, ultimately, perform at a higher level. You do this through applying coaching principles.

Be flexible and consistent: Being flexible means releasing preconceived solutions to problems to open the way to your staffers exploring their issues. During their exploration, you might discover there are better ways of addressing the situation than the one you had in mind.

Stay the course, knowing that change requires more than one conversation. Coaching continuity reinforces and sustains growth. Whether it's a five-minute coaching conversation or your regular meeting, continue the process to see results.

Aim for a coaching culture through your consistency. Though every conversation doesn't require coaching, in as much as possible apply the style regularly, through both quick problem-solving interactions and structured, scheduled one-on-ones.

Not every conversation benefits from coaching. There are times when being directive is best, such as when time constraints dictate faster decision-making.

Prepare to be more silent: Using a *coaching leader* method means learning to be silent more often. Listening is a powerful coaching skill, much more useful than non-stop talking. Your input should be intentional, limited, and meaningful, mostly interjecting good questions to help move the conversation along a path that enables direct reports to identify their next actions. Resist the urge to jump in early to provide answers.

Let go of fixing people. Remember, coaching assumes people have the most knowledge and resources to solve their problems. Help them do that. Paraphrasing something I came across: "*Coaching isn't about stepping in and doing your team member's work. It is about helping them be more effective so they can do the work without you standing over them.*"

Think about the micro-managing to under-managing spectrum: Coaching enables a balance between hands-on and hands-off leadership. Micromanaging as a style is constraining for you and your team. **Leaders' styles tend to waver**

between over and under-management. Neither is ideal; coaching allows you to achieve a better balance.

Micro- or over-management is the tendency of fearful, commanding leaders to be controlling about their direct reports' work and processes. Some of the signs: *requiring every task be approved by you, being copied on every email, having to know your staff whereabouts at all times, re-doing their work, and hardly ever delegating tasks.*

This kind of management creates a debilitating environment that smothers creativity, fosters dependency, immobilizes action, and instills anxiety. During the few occasions when I worked under a micro-managing leader, my thought was, "If you're doing my job, who's doing yours? In fact, what is yours?"

Micro-managers justify themselves with statements like[37]:

- ✓ It saves time for me to just do it myself.
- ✓ Too much is at stake to allow this to go wrong.
- ✓ My credibility is on the line if it's not done right.
- ✓ When I'm not involved, they are sure to mess things up.

At the other end of the spectrum is the hands-off manager, and that's not ideal either. Some people love the idea of a hands-off manager, at least initially. They experience freedom and autonomy, but eventually realize they are lacking challenge,

---

[37] Wilkins, M. Signs that you're a micromanager, *HBR*, Nov. 2014

support or growth. Further, your direct reports suffer from inattention and little strategic focus to their work. When the hands-off manager is complacent and lacks vision, there is little advocacy and mentoring for their employees. Being led by this type leads to disengagement, boredom, and career stagnation.

A story of extremes. *"Following a horrid experience with a micro-manager who made my life stressful, I was ecstatic to work with my new manager who basically said, 'You know your work. Do it the way that works best and I'll check in when we have our bi-weekly meeting.' Yippee! I loved this until about six months in. I was bored, directionless and felt stuck because I had no mentor, no learning, no champion... just a complacent supervisor who was content to just do her job the same way over and over. I began to dread going to work because I felt rudderless. In the end, I don't know which type was worst- micro or no management."* Millennial HR advisor

The coach-leader is a third and better path. It's not over or under-management; it's providing what each direct report needs using a coaching framework.

3. Apply a coaching framework

During coaching conversations, the direct reports provide most of the session goals, and you provide a process that helps them grow. You might help your team members define some of the goals (especially related to their performance metrics).

Generally, though, the session goals belong to them along with how they think they can best achieve them.

A basic framework for supervisory coaching. It's *a framework—not a strict, scripted process*. The model below offers you a mental model that can lead to greater awareness, discovery and transformation for your staff. It draws from the GROW[38] model and the FUEL[39] framework.

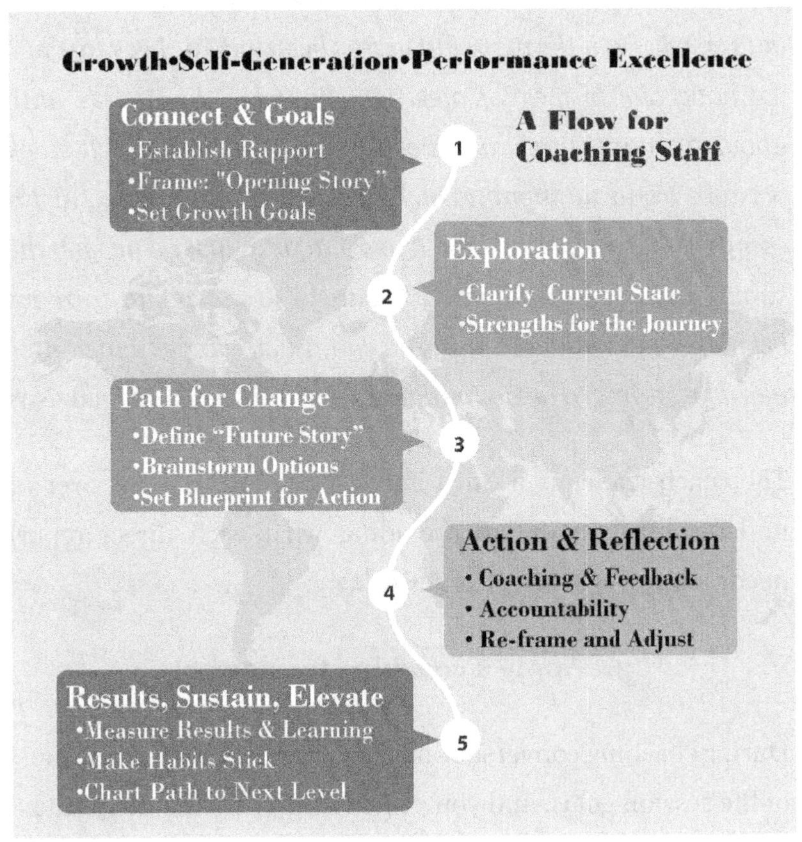

---

[38] Created by Sir John Whitmore in 1980
[39] From Zenger and Stinnett, *The Extraordinary Coach.*

Here are examples of the types of questions for each step.

Description	Simple Guiding Questions (or use similar ones in your words)
❶ After building **rapport**, here you set the **goal**, or learn what your staffer is trying to achieve and why it's important (short- or longer-term)	*What's the goal you'd like to achieve? What topic do you want to talk about? What's the most important thing we should spend our time on? What makes this important for you?*
❷ Now together, **explore** to get a better picture of what's happening right now and what's been tried	*Briefly, what's been happening? Can you help me better understand what you are facing? What have you tried so far? Which of your current strengths have you used for this? What are the obstacles? Is it a realistic goal?*
❸ Brainstorm a range of **options** (supervisor may add to these), choose the best options, set **time-bound actions** and what success would look like when the goal is achieved	*What can you do to accomplish this? What else? Which option makes the most sense for you? If you do these things, what do you think will be different? What are you committed to doing next to achieve the goal? What's your timeline? What support can I give to help you be effective?*
❹ **Ongoing** coaching, check **accountability** for action steps, **reflect** on progress, **adjust** actions as needed.	Check in on action steps and progress; repeat steps 2-4 as needed. *Can we check in on progress? Can we walk through your actions steps and how things went? What worked? What didn't? How do you feel about the progress? What's next?*
❺ **Celebrate** the growth, **Sustain** the change achieved, then define next, **elevated** growth goals.	*Let's spend some time reflecting on your success in addressing your goals. What will you do to sustain the changes you've made? What is your next level of growth? How can I support you?*

Three Examples (of applying a coaching method):

Here are examples to illustrate coaching in action. These are not full conversations; they are meant to emphasize the leader's use of questions (rather than lots of telling), then listening intently to walk the direct report through to their next steps.

Example #1: On the spot problem solving.

Quick coaching

Employee: "In 15 minutes, I've got a meeting with my colleague who has been defensive every time we talk. Can you offer me some tips?"

Leader: (allow employee to respond to the questions). Can you quickly share the typical situation? Can you think of ways you are interacting that seem to have set him off? So, what might be one to two things you can do a bit differently when you go in there to make it a better interaction? Give it a try. I think your ideas are sound (unless the ideas clearly won't work; then offer a tip). Let's talk more afterward.

Example #2: Ongoing one-on-ones for performance support.

Performance Support

Leader questions: "Since we're at the start of a new quarter, I'd love to hear how you're progressing so far this year."

Can you review your goals and describe how you think you're progressing? What are you especially proud of? What is a change you'd like to make to achieve your goals by year-end? How would that make your work more successful? What are some things you could do to get better in that area? Which make the most sense and you'd really commit to? How can I help? What are the first/next steps?

Example #3: Coaching for development/growth.

Development and Growth

"So, I know you wanted to talk about some career goals you have in mind. Let's use some of our time looking forward at those goals. Is this a good time?"

So, how exactly would you like to grow in your work, let's say over the next one to two years? Great, tell me what makes this the path you want to pursue. What things have you already done to prepare? What do you think pursuing this growth will require? What might you do to get started? How can I support you? When do you want to check in again on the actions you've agreed to take?

Practice Activity: Consider everyday situations you face with those who report to you. Think about how you can apply a coaching strategy in one of those situations. Maybe something like: "Can we debrief the new hire meeting you lead last week?" Or "Can we talk about how you are working to build a better partnership with your colleague?" or "I'd like to hear your ideas to address the low achievement of the three students in your class" or "I'd like us to talk about the reports that were due two days ago." Or....

a) How might you prepare for this conversation?

b) What do you need to pay attention to as you have the conversation?

Coaching shifted thinking: *"I came in thinking about myself and finished thinking bigger--about my Whys and the Whys of others."* –short-term coachee, age 28, tech specialist

4. From telling and advising to listening and inquiring

It will be an adjustment for some to stop talking so much, and instead, listen deeply to guide your staffers to becoming more resourceful and capable. Few employees have the opportunity to explore their thinking to help them arrive at new insights. You can provide them that opening as a coaching leader.

Listening goes beyond hearing. It requires letting go of preconceived answers, which leaders tend to have about what people should be and do. Listen for words, emotions, and alterations in thinking so you can, through thoughtful follow-up questions, prompt your people to discover new possibilities.

Spending time asking quality questions should not seem like an interrogation. Your aim is not to listen to respond but rather to understand fully. And, since coaching is more easily described than executed, you want to get good at inquiry, so as issues arise, you can sense which questions might deepen, redirect, or expand your staff's thinking.

When assuming your coaching leader role, your speaking functions are largely asking, summarizing, and sharing observations. Most of the time should belong to your direct report (think 75%), while you listen to hear what's said and what's not. Your input is largely *listening* to prompt better inquiry, using good questions, *summarizing* and paraphrasing to reflect back what you've heard. Wait until after the direct report has explored their own thinking in depth to occasionally offer your *observations*. They don't need you to rescue them but will appreciate your occasional observations. **The graphic below represents your four basic coaching inputs.**

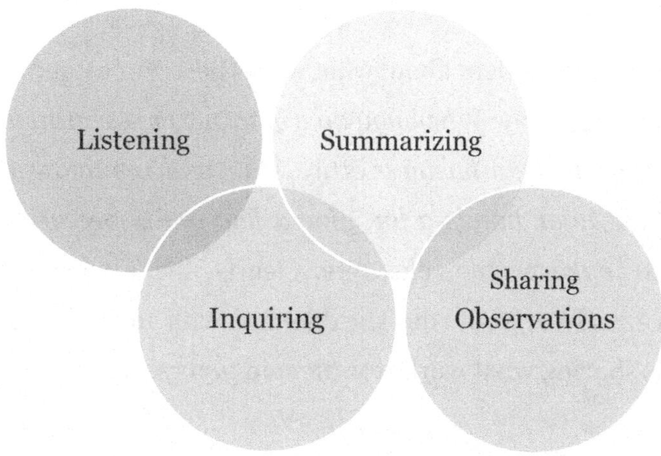

Coaching impacts personal life too. Two direct reports each shared with me the difference coaching made with their teenaged sons. Both staffers began to do more asking about their son's thoughts; in both cases, the sons were surprised and seemed awkward at first. *What do you want to accomplish today? Huh?* After a few days of questions, he said *I want to complete... talk to my teacher about*...etc. Same story with the other father with his two adult sons. He learned to ask and not tell, informally coach and not boss his adult sons. He observed a newfound patience which this required of him and the positive results and the reduced defensiveness of his sons.

So, what about advice? It has a place, when used sparingly.

> *"The principal danger of advice giving is that it can be a self-administered aphrodisiac, doing more to satisfy your ego than to help your client [direct report]... so whatever advice you give, be brief."*[40]

Advice means giving ideas about what works best. For example, a supervisor might say: *When you give your next presentation it's always best to wear business attire, start with a humorous anecdote, use your hands a lot, give a few self-deprecating remarks to make people relax,* etc. Clearly, that's what the person giving advice would do. The dilemma with advice is that the giver is sharing what works for *them* in *your* situation.

---

[40] Bacon, T. and Spear, K. *Adaptive Coaching*, 2012, p. 198

Will Smith summarized it well in *Will*, his 2021 memoir: "*Advice, at its best, is one person's limited perspective of the infinite possibilities before you. People's advice is based on their fears, their experiences, their prejudices. At the end of the day, their advice is just that, theirs not yours.*" (p. 99)

The well-intentioned advice giver generally fails to consider what might work for the other person's style, background, mindset, etc. And, if anyone reading this has teenagers, what typically happens when you give advice? They, at best, pretend to listen, then they act on *their* instincts and thought process.

Asking for, but not needing, my advice. I recall a coaching client insisting he needed my opinion (another word for advice). I asked him to think his challenge through, and he came up with nothing. He wanted to know what I would do, so I then said: "I don't think giving my own advice is best, however, what I've seen people do in the situation you're facing is to do this or that, etc." What did he say? "No, that won't work; I think I'd be better doing xyz." .... Advice wasn't very helpful.

When your staffers present scenarios that may have them stuck, use questions such as: *Can you take a moment and think about some possible options? In similar situations, what have you tried that might work? What attributes or strengths do you have that might be helpful in this situation?*

As a coaching-leader, encourage team members to brainstorm with you, to create a list of options; some may be good, some may be not so good. Usually, the person comes up with at least an option or two that you likely would not have given them; they come up with options that suit their style and background. Will these options work? They'd have to try them to know that. You can agree to check back a few days after they've tried their best option and talk through what worked and what didn't.

When is advice useful? There are occasions when advice is helpful. Some of those could be: 1) when the person has a limited repertoire of experience to draw upon, 2) when they ask directly; though be brief and refrain from advice that comes totally from your experience, 3) to help staffers explore alternative paths (which is not the same as specific advice), 4) when your direct report is planning their goals and actions and you want to be sure their plans line up with performance expectations. In this case, to keep the work focused and on track to high performance, there should be specific, direct and often non-negotiable goals or tasks and 5) occasionally, when there is no time for processing approaches; later, you'll want to share the reasoning behind your advice in that situation.

And yes, I've given advice and you will too—based on the circumstances. On occasion, and after the person has explored their options, I may give advice if they still believe they need it. You might put the advice in the form of a question, such as: *Your plan seems solid; would it help if you wrote down what specifically you are going to say to Jim before going in?*

30 sample coaching questions. Here are 30 questions for your use or to stimulate you to generate your own. These are largely open-ended questions which enable people to interrogate their own thinking, gain insight and draw better conclusions. Do not use *pretend* coaching questions (those with built in biases or that suggest a right answer) or questions that don't sound natural coming from you. For more ideas, there are plenty of leader-coach questions on the Internet.

☑ Check any of these coaching questions that could work for you:

1. What's the main thing to make our time most valuable today?
2. What would you like to leave our conversation with?
3. What do you think is at the core of this issue? (the cause)
4. What has worked well before that you might build on?
5. To get the best results, what would you do differently or better?
6. What are some choices for addressing the situation?
7. What would you like to leave our conversation with?
8. What's to gain or lose in your proposed scenario?
9. Are there other ways you can look at this?
10. If you brought the best of yourself to this situation, what would that look like?
11. In what ways do you think you contributed to this situation?
12. What can you do to create the very best outcome possible?
13. What else? What else? Anything else?

14. What do you believe makes you think about it that way?
15. Who will be affected by this option? Harmed by it?
16. What excites you most about this?
17. What impact is this situation having on you? On anyone else?
18. What did you consider doing, but didn't?
19. What's at stake with each option?
20. What are you trading off if you take that course?
21. How do you feel about your options?
22. What are the benefits that make it worth the risk (if any)?
23. Can I offer a few more options for you to consider?
24. Which of your strengths can you engage to help address this?
25. What if you do nothing?
26. What could you be missing or avoiding?
27. How have you successfully handled similar situations before?
28. Will this get you where you and the organization need to go?
29. What might get in the way as you follow your action plan?
30. What are the very first steps you will take to be more successful?

Use of closed-ended questions when coaching. There are, at times, advantages to using closed-ended questions (those with a direct Yes or No or when there is a small set of options for specific responses). *The power of a closed-ended question lies in its ability to help the direct report be definitive, make a clear choice, confirm commitment, i.e., get to the* *bottom line.* Examples of powerful closed-ended questions when coaching your direct reports include: *Is this something you are really committed to act on? When will you do this? Who is responsible? Is that the best use of your time?*

Practice using questions that are appropriate for the situation. They should not be disruptive to the flow of the conversation, and they should feel seamless, logical, genuine and natural.

A case of an un-powerful question. This happened during one early conversation with an effusive, affable client. After 10 minutes of his steady flow of words, he said "Does that make sense?" without pausing for an answer. He did this twice more before I gently interrupted (as he took a breath). I asked whether he was aware of his habit of asking that question which didn't seem to be seeking a response. As we explored this habit, which he often used with his direct reports, I asked him what he wanted that question to do for him. He had no answer. He realized it was nervous insecurity rather than a genuine request for input. How can you make it more effective? He responded: *Use it less frequently. Pause if I really am seeking input.* After doing that, his staffers began sharing their thoughts, which they hadn't before. This improvement pleased them and him.

5. Become a master of providing quality feedback

Coaching, generally speaking, is developmental and *future-focused* regarding employee performance. Another application of the coaching style is to provide quality feedback, information of *past behavior*, both positive and corrective. Unlike developmental proactive coaching (with its future-focus), feedback coaching shines a light on *past* behaviors and supports direct reports in determining what behaviors should be continued and which may need redirection.

Feedback is simply *information* that helps us know if our actions are 'on track', whether we are moving closer to or further away from our target.[41] There are three main types: *reinforcing* (confirming, positive), *redirecting* (disconfirming, corrective), *and none* (neglect).

Everyone needs feedback regularly and well-executed. Unfortunately, many leaders' beliefs and insecurities interfere with their ability to give (and receive) feedback. Some fear providing feedback, or they offer it so poorly that it fails to accomplish what good feedback can. Some worry that feedback won't land well, so it's withheld. Others, wait until they build up a list of infractions before sharing it, resulting in hard feelings. Then there are those who, even in the face of positive behaviors, withhold confirming feedback. Still others withhold feedback of any kind, whether direct reports are doing well or not so well. *This display of indifference is the worst approach to feedback.*

---

[41] Zenger & Stinnett, *The Extraordinary Coach*, P. 199

Developing your feedback muscle will give you greater value to your direct reports.

Reflection: Beliefs and intention matter. Take a few moments to explore your thinking about giving and receiving feedback.

1. What are you feedback habits (whether offering positive or corrective information)?

2. What beliefs might be holding you back from giving more positive feedback?

3. What attitude might be holding you back from giving more corrective feedback?

4. What, generally, are your intentions when giving feedback?

5. What is a recent situation in which you wanted to give better, more useful feedback? (Keep this example in mind as you review how to improve feedback skills.)

The consequences of no or poor feedback. Since providing staffers with abundant, quality feedback is crucial to their performance and satisfaction, withholding it can sound like: *"Wow, if I had known I would have addressed that sooner, rather than keep doing the same thing."*

Downside of receiving no redirecting feedback. *"I wasn't performing well in a role. This was frustrating because my supervisor seemed uninterested in my success. This supervisor would not or could not give me actionable information to help improve my performance – very frustrating. Fortunately, a mentor was able to give me enough feedback about my blind spots, which enabled me to turn things around."* –Interviewee, mid-level leader

In my work with leaders and colleagues who've reported being stunned when placed on a performance improvement plan or released, it's like a mantra: *"I had no idea that the way I was working with (fill in name or group) was that problematic."* My response: *Didn't you receive feedback long before now?* Their reply went something like this: *No, not really. I heard something once months ago, but not since. So, I thought things had improved.* The feedback was either missing or not provided well. And there was likely a bit of the leader's refusal to face the truth or inability to read the handwriting on the *wall.* This makes effective feedback even more important, even when it hurts.

Confirming feedback boosts motivation. A mid-level, 30-something leader revealed she received feedback at the close of her first two weeks on the job. Her leader let her know what a great hire she was, then went on to give specifics about what she'd seen so far: *You offer great ideas, your skill in building systems and tools is sorely needed in our department, your way of giving ideas to push my thinking makes you worth your weight in gold*, etc. Then, an added surprise was when the leader asked: *Am I making your experience a great one? Do I move too fast? Do you feel you have what you need so far? What else can I do?* Afterward, the direct report said she was ready to give even more to do her job very well.

Tips on providing quality feedback:

- ☑ Reorient yourself around the *benefits* of feedback.
- ☑ Remember, feedback is ongoing. Behavior change requires many conversations. Habits are pesky, but not irreversible. So, keep at it, acknowledging incremental growth.
- ☑ Know it's a two-way process, a conversation that includes good advocacy and inquiry to foster better understanding and best actions going forward.
- ☑ All feedback should be about behavior, not the person.
- ☑ The more trusting the relationship (the CONNECT key), the more likely the feedback will be valued.
- ☑ Be specific about the behavior and the *Why*—its impact on the job or people (whether positive or corrective feedback).
- ☑ Provide it in a timely manner. Set aside a private time for more complex or difficult feedback.

- ☑ Apply balanced feedback, that is, more positive than corrective. An ideal ratio is at least 3:1 (positive/corrective)
- ☑ Practice and build comfort giving feedback regularly.

A general feedback process: Below is an example of how to give good feedback developed by a group of mid-level leaders. There are many books that address feedback, so think of theirs as a non-scientific, but good, example.

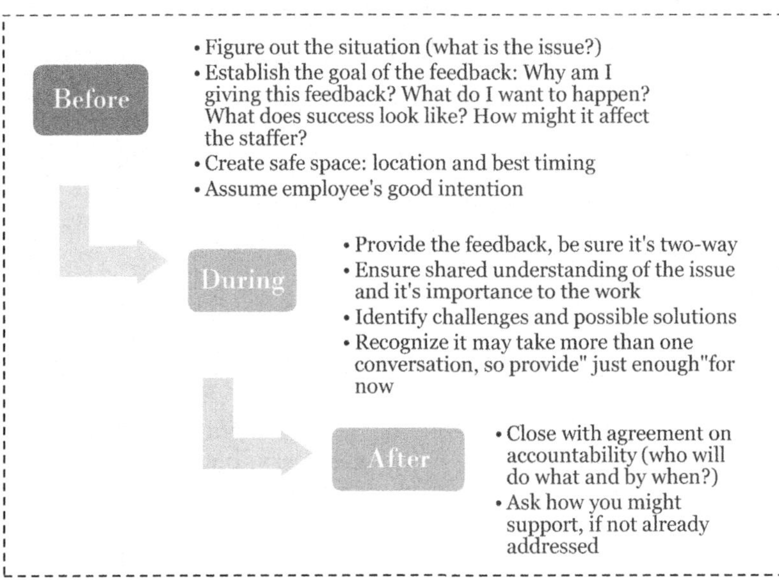

Before
• Figure out the situation (what is the issue?)
• Establish the goal of the feedback: Why am I giving this feedback? What do I want to happen? What does success look like? How might it affect the staffer?
• Create safe space: location and best timing
• Assume employee's good intention
During
• Provide the feedback, be sure it's two-way
• Ensure shared understanding of the issue and it's importance to the work
• Identify challenges and possible solutions
• Recognize it may take more than one conversation, so provide" just enough"for now
After
• Close with agreement on accountability (who will do what and by when?)
• Ask how you might support, if not already addressed

A feedback example

Feedback

"I'd like to get your thoughts on how the project is going, and then, I'd like to share and get your reaction to some feedback."

Sample conversation questions*: Can you review the project goals? What's worked well? Where did you get stuck (if at all)? What are you thinking about doing differently?*

Here are a few thoughts on what I observed... (share what went well and what can be improved).

	Any reactions? (Listen to understand before responding). *So, what things will you do to move forward on the project to help ensure its success? In what ways do you need my support?*

Taking Action for Better Coaching: Below, list four behaviors, actions or attitudes you commit to take related to applying a coaching style to help maximize the performance and satisfaction of your staffers.

Action, Behavior or Attitude tasks	Timeline to start
1.	
2.	
3.	
4.	

This closes *Chapter 12, The Coach Key*. Chapter 13 builds on coaching as it looks at other ways to Develop your direct reports' talents and skills to enhance performance and grow their careers.

Developing your people has wide-reaching benefits. As you commit to their growth, you grow, results grow, and they stay and grow with you longer.

Chapter 13
The DEVELOP Key

In the previous chapter, coaching was touted as a key differentiator and competency for high-performing *people-leaders*. Chapter 13 explores a range of activities, in addition to coaching, that DEVELOP those you are leading.

The topics are: 1) Develop people to unlock and grow talents, 2) development options, 3) embed learning into your meeting culture, 4) delegate for growth, and 5) support well-being.

1. Develop people to unlock and grow talents

To develop staff means to be deliberate about sharpening their technical skills and enhancing professional behaviors (e.g., communication, adaptability, collaboration, etc.). Improving skills increases your direct reports' value to the organization and contributes to higher staff satisfaction. The best leaders engage in on-going learning and development for themselves and their team members using a variety of methods. The leader plans methods to continually enhance their and the staff team's mindset, behaviors and skills. These efforts foster increased motivation and engagement, improved performance and career progress. Then, regarding the elusive issue of how to retain high-value staff, investing in developing them encourages people to stay with an organization. Additionally, when leaders give priority to developing their staff members, they are able to confidently delegate tasks, allowing them to redirect their resources to the organization's higher-level work.

Ask yourself: *Am I, as the leader...*

- ☑ *aware of the discrepancy between current skills and needed skills for effectiveness for each of my direct reports?*
- ☑ *one who provides ongoing positive feedback so direct reports are aware of their skills and motivated to further develop them?*
- ☑ *an ongoing learner who champions the same for my team?*
- ☑ *an encourager and provider of ways for team members to learn new or better skills and to mature professionally?*
- ☑ *someone who creates and follows my own development plan and does the same for each direct report?*
- ☑ *a supporter of the organization's succession planning evident by preparing my direct reports to advance in the organization?*
- ☑ *keeping team members abreast of trends in their current and next level area of work?*

Begin to examine avenues to answer Yes to these questions, and some of those only require minimal expense.

2. Range of development options

In today's workplace, your direct reports may be co-located, geographically dispersed or in a hybrid setting. These newer ways of working offer opportunities to learn and develop in a variety of ways. The graphic below highlights some of the methods for engaging your team in growth-oriented learning. Many cost very little. So even when finances are constrained, there's no reason to neglect professional development.

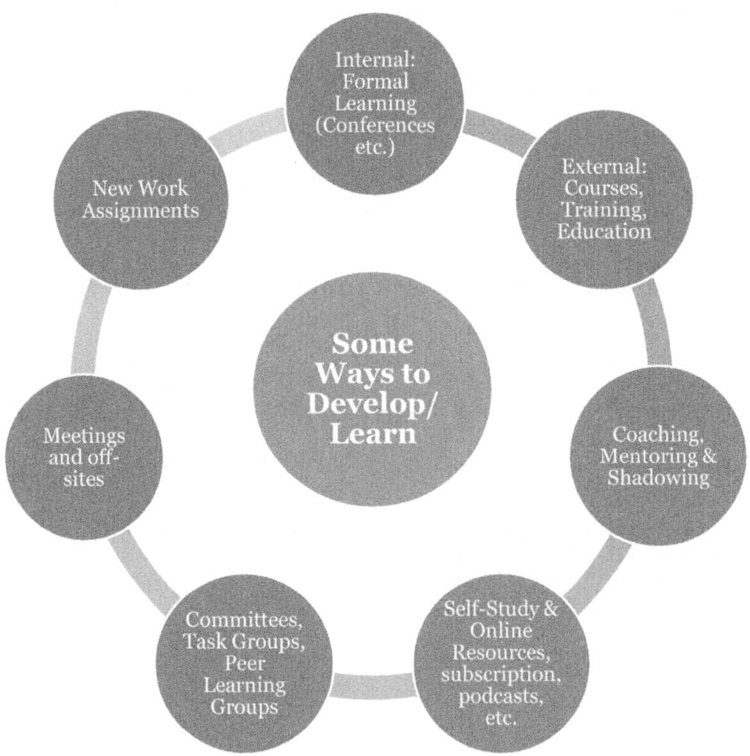

Think about these options for developing your direct reports: New or expanded work assignments, opportunities to lead an initiative or group, shadowing someone to learn new or better systems or skills, appointment to committees, joining topical peer learning groups, one-on-one coaching, mini or multi-day conferences, job rotations, in-meeting learning blocks, certifications and degree attainment, reading groups, mentoring or teaching others (which hones own skills, while creating new processes and launching new initiatives).

What are some other ways to grow your team members' skills?

____

____

Development Activity: Take a few minutes to 1) reflect on your direct reports' existing skills, attributes, hobbies, etc. 2) Next consider which skills or qualities are needed to achieve some of the team or organization goals, 3) Now, using the table below, jot down a few notes on how you might engage your staff in value-adding growth opportunities (conferences, special assignments, shadowing, etc.).

Your suggestions are starting points. Gather ideas from your direct reports since you are making decisions *with* them, not *for* them. Proactively sharing your ideas about their growth can be heartening for staffers. *"I was thinking about you and know you have potential to accomplish some exciting things that can help the organization in the near future. I'd like to share them with you and also hear your ideas, even if yours are different or areas that you are more passionate about."*

Name	Growth area	Development method(s)

Leader's Development Story. *"I always asked direct reports what they wanted from me as their leader, then I was intentional about developing a plan for them. It was great watching staff grow and develop in response to the plan. However, the difficult part is letting go of those who are ready for the next step in their career."* --F. Gill, NP executive

3. Embed learning into your meeting culture

One way to develop skills among your direct reports is by planning and facilitating better meetings. Since meetings consume a lot of time, and many lack engagement or clear purpose, you can score a win by shifting the culture and quality of your meetings.

Better meetings can reduce or get rid of common poor meeting outcomes. Some of these include feeling time is wasted, false consensus (when people just go along), acceptance of silence as a form of agreement (when it's not), and unfocused agendas that lead to more confusion than clarity and decision-making.

Two powerful ways to ensure better, results-oriented meetings (See Chapter 9 for more suggestions.)

1. ***Establish meeting norms***, ensuring a better meeting culture. You and your team can do this at any time or when you develop a team charter (addressed in Chapter 9). Collectively chosen meeting principles (also called norms or agreements) will transform both quality and satisfaction. Don't be shocked when your team begins looking forward to meetings, finding them purposeful and enjoyable. They will assume the decision to meet means there's some meat on the bones, and they have a part in it.

   Below are some examples of meeting norms pulled from work and consultations, adopted based on a team's needs:

   a. All agendas will include a clear purpose, desired outcomes and follow-up actions.

b. Once monthly, meetings will provide *nutrition* for the mind, body and spirit/emotions—our whole selves.

c. We make time on the agenda for sharing, problem solving and innovation (more than updates).

d. Agendas should be structured, flexible and engaging.

e. We share the lead for planning and executing meetings.

f. Longer meetings will be preceded by pre-stimulation, such as pre-reads, learning circles or short videos.

g. Meetings will provide space and time for group work and individual reflection (unless time constrained).

h. Various approaches and mediums are used to present and engage participants.

i. Participant experiences are valued, and their expertise integrated into our meeting activities.

j. Plan meetings that are enjoyable, include breaks and ways to have fun.

k. Meetings will start and end on time, with a summary and next steps at the end.

l. Meetings are clearly connected over time, so they actually take us somewhere.

One change made a difference. An email I received read... *You said that we need to ask ourselves: "What is the purpose of this meeting?" I learned I need to be more intentional in the planning of meetings, and that statement really resonated with me. Today my board chair and I are planning our board agenda and I'm going to add a purpose statement to the official agenda. I think that will keep us more focused."* —nonprofit mid-level executive

2. ***Embed learning:*** One powerful method to bring more interest, dynamism and purpose to your existing meetings is to embed learning into them. You might carve out 20 minutes for bursts of learning around topics of importance to the team and the organization. These can be identified by the team (and you) and can be added to an annual meeting schedule. Ask each team member to select and lead one learning topic from the list, allowing you to share leadership.

   You can ask at your annual launch meeting: What should be our priority areas for learning to enhance our work? Then when you start this practice, make sure it's done well.

   To dig into the learning topic, include a brief pre-thinking activity. Team members might choose an article, a book chapter, podcast to view in advance, a virtual short chat with an expert, etc. Simple questions to guide the learning might be: *What were the two biggest ideas? What meaning does this learning piece have for how we do our work? Is there one nugget you would take away and integrate into your thinking or your work?* What makes this robust is the sharing out and comparing the thoughts in the room and learning from this sharing.

A word about Off-sites (retreats). Committing the time and resources for staff off-sites (single or multi-day) ought to be the result of good planning and foster both building team bonds and enhancing learning. (The Appendix offers guidance to help you make these high-cost events transformational, high-value development initiatives.)

4. Delegate for growth

Delegation is an often-neglected development approach, especially when you're a high-engagement, multi-tasking (and micro-managing) leader. Skillful delegation develops staff competencies, and the leader frees up their time to do more of the strategic work compatible with their organizational level.

> *"Somebody noted to me that by the time something reaches my desk, that means it's really hard. Because if it were easy, somebody else would have made the decision and somebody else would have solved it."* –Barack Obama

Though delegation is a powerful avenue for development, some leaders view keeping everything close to them as a badge of honor. Below are some typical rationales leaders offer for not delegating as they spend endless hours doing many tasks (some are known to gloat over their *over-dedication* to work).

Managers' greatest obstacles to delegation	
Belief that *I can do it better myself*	Unskilled at knowing how or what to delegate
Fear loss of control, low-risk taker, insecure	Believe it's too time consuming to prepare people
Lack of confidence in staff	Attachment to previous responsibilities; hard time letting go

Delegation *is the transfer of responsibility and ownership from a leader to a direct report*. It allows both the leader and others to increase their productivity. Delegation is a low-cost means to develop and inspire staff as communicated in the interviewee's comments below.

New project assignment inspires. *"One of my most rewarding experiences was working collaboratively with my supervisor on a major project. It made me feel as though my supervisor trusted my work. It also did a lot for my confidence and willingness to take on more projects."* —interviewee, university manager

So, what does effective delegation look like? Delegation is a thoughtful process that goes beyond just giving a task away and expecting the direct report to be exceptional at it.

It begins with your readiness: First, work towards a mindset that delegation is helpful and can be done well. Relinquish the thought that assignments have to be done exactly as you do them. Consider instead the outcomes to be achieved as your direct reports put their talents to work on the tasks. Also, keep at it; things probably won't be perfect the first time.

A Delegation Process (Summary of Steps)
(followed by brief descriptions of the seven steps)

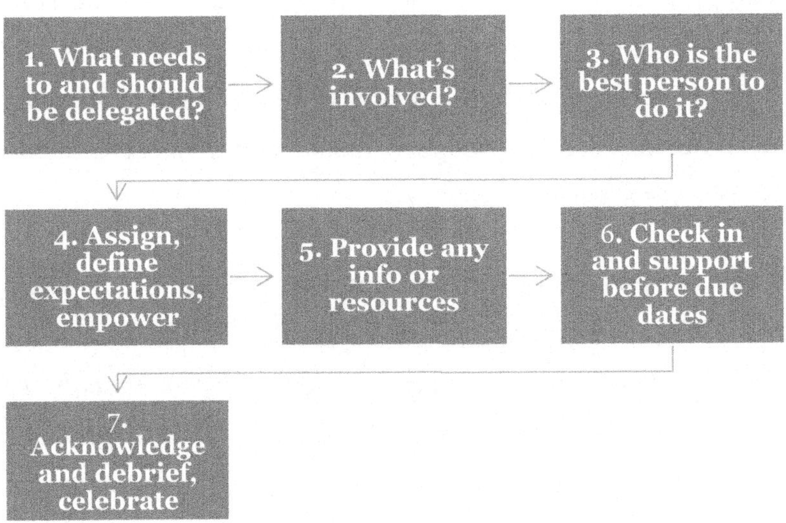

1. Decide **what needs to, should, and can be delegated**. Consider what you can take off of your list to elevate the work of your direct reports. These may be tasks you have performed over the years or new priorities.

2. For each assignment you are delegating, be sure **of what's involved** in completing the tasks. Are there steps, people, skills, processes, time requirements, etc. that will be needed to take on the task? Identify them.

3. Determine **who is the best person** to take on each task. Think through the best alignment with your direct reports' specific strengths, suitability for the task, their motivation to grow their work and career, their availability, how they can make the time, and their career goals.

4. Offer or **make the assignment, define expectations,** any specifications and boundaries, then empower them. Make this a positive experience for the direct report, sharing your belief in their abilities and your support for their growth. Communicate why the task is important, what it requires, timelines, etc. Then advise them regarding their level of autonomy with the assignment (empowerment).

5. **Provide them with the resources** to carry out the tasks. That might include existing documents, prior materials or processes related to the project, introductions to people, tools, training, etc.

6. Establish **check-in times** to share progress, challenges and provide support BEFORE completion dates. This is critical because delegation failure is more likely when the leader waits until the deadline to see how things turned out.

7. Finally, **acknowledge completion, debrief, celebrate** what went very well and share only a few suggestions for continuous improvement. After the direct report has completed the delegated task once or a few times, you will likely not need to check in as much but determine together what that check in cadence should be.

Remember, there's a lot of power in effectively delegating. It demonstrates your belief in your team members' abilities and it helps them grow, and you as well.

5. Support well-being practices

One final area about the DEVELOP key, which was introduced in Chapter 7, is giving attention to your direct reports' well-being. How people carry out their work is greatly influenced by the state of their well-being. You want your team to bring the best of themselves to work, so consider how to support them in building emotional agility, warding off burnout, and preserving or developing healthier mental and physical states.

Consider your and others' various areas of life as you think about well-being. This covers things such as feelings of belonging, balance, level of energy, emotional/spiritual states, moods, stress levels, outside relaxing pursuits, feelings of safety, sense of hopefulness, physical wellness, family and friendship, lifestyle practices and hobbies, and other items.

Work life balance (or integration) has been a theme in the forefront for decades, and many employers and employees have yet to figure it out. As a developmental, growth-promoting leader, support and encourage staff with balancing the range of choices available for their well-being.

Without being overly intrusive, you can demonstrate your caring about the whole person for each direct report by periodically checking in on well-being practices. As a leader and a coach, it's a matter of standard practice for me to ask questions such as: *So, how are you ensuring your overall well-being at work and home? What practices have proven best for you? How do you regenerate, refresh and renew your energy?*

In response to these type queries, people may share lifestyle practices about nutrition, exercise, hobbies, travel, quiet time, outdoor adventure, communing with nature, and such. Checking in can make a difference; it shows you realize you are working with and care about real, whole, human beings. And clients have stated that being asked reminds them to attend to non-work pursuits that refresh and renew them.

Life is not just work, but life affects work. Know that, like you, people are in the middle of other things besides work, and they may bring emotional residuals to work. So, to lead others well and to develop them, showing concern and encouraging well-being activities, even making work adjustments, matters.

Closing reflection What one to three ideas from this chapter resonated most for you? Which will you examine further or act on to be better at DEVELOPING your team members?

1.

2.

3.

This closes *Chapter 13, The Develop Key*. Spend time on a few of the ideas addressed in the chapter. Then take steps to be better at developing all of your team members, which benefits them, the organization and you.

Ultimately the role of the leader, whether at work or with volunteers, is to evoke the required performance from those they are leading in service to accomplishing meaningful objectives.

Chapter 14
The PERFORM Key

A leader's work all comes down to this—*leading your direct reports to achieve the required results at work— Performance.* Caring for your team, good processes, coaching, staff development, great retreats, and positive incentives bring value when they are clear *line of sight* activities—linking directly to those in your charge accomplishing quality results. These are means to an end, not the end itself.

The leader's big question is: *How can I hire, inspire, develop and retain staff who consistently achieve our shared goals?* The PERFORM key is what ties all of our efforts together. It's the reason we hire people and recruit volunteers, and why we lead initiatives—to *achieve* something meaningful.

What are the best approaches to inspire good performance? Is it berating and browbeating people into performing or working in a performance culture that blends caring and accountability? If you think about what you'd want for yourself, you'd agree the latter has the greatest possibility of evoking quality and sustained work results. Today's top workplaces are those that trust people will perform well in an environment that is simultaneously humane, satisfying, challenging, and accountability-focused.

Chapter 14 looks at five topics for leading people to PERFORM masterfully: 1) Performance goal clarity and accountability, 2) setting a cadence of goal checkpoints, 3) aligning recognition with performance, 4) better appraisal meetings, and 5) performance-based transitions: up, over or out.

To perform means *to achieve or exceed value-adding and required organizational (business) results. These results are achieved in a way consistent with the cultural standards and values of the organization.*

Here are some questions to ask yourself about the PERFORM key. Place a check (✓) on those you already do. Circle those that are areas of opportunity for you.

1. *Do I set goals in partnership with my direct reports?*
2. *Do I try out different methods to motivate people to perform?*
3. *Do I provide clear, measurable goals so there is little chance of misinterpretation?*

4. *Do team members have the opportunity to share their view of their performance and their needs?*

5. *Am I skilled at balancing empathy with the expectation of accountability?*

6. *Am I flexible with appraising performance when environmental factors create barriers to achieving expected performance?*

7. *Am I fair and unbiased in appraising all of my direct reports?*

8. *Do I act courageously and decisively when addressing chronic low performance?*

9. *Do I provide quality rewards and incentives for achieving desired performance year-round and annually?*

10. *Do I have a rhythm of check-ins with direct reports on progress, status, support needs and challenges related to achieving goals?*

1. Performance goal clarity and accountability

When setting, reinforcing and evaluating performance, be sure both you, as the supervising leader, and the direct report have the same clarity. One of the performance gaps I've witnessed, notably when coaching a leader facing performance challenges, is related to vagueness about the goals and what the specific standards are for low, average or high performance.

Colleagues who are performance management experts often see a good bit of discordance between the leader's and their direct reports' view of performance. The causes of the discrepancy range from vaguely written goals, poor or no communication through the evaluation period, unrealistic goals (without considering staffer's workload and work conditions), to goals being created by the supervisor without input from the person being evaluated.

"My performance score was unexpected." Two mid-level leaders asked my thoughts about the same scenario. Both received lower than expected scores on annual reviews. Both had always gotten *exceeds expectations* over the past several years. Midway through the performance year, each experienced a change in manager. Without conversation, the new managers each separately decided they'd provide their own performance appraisal. What was the cause of the difference? Why couldn't these staffers *predict* their performance based on their work products? Had these newly-installed managers exploited their *manager power*?

To elicit the best performance, pay attention to how you conduct goal setting. Consider the following:

- **Prepare goals jointly**. Remember the direct report is closest to the actual job responsibilities and likely has ideas on how to optimize their effectiveness. You may have a reason to modify or stretch the goals they recommend; if so, ensure there's a common understanding of your rationale (since you want your staff to own the goals and be *motivated* to achieve them).

- **Be clear on how performance will be measured**. Is there a scale that determines the extent to which standards of achievement are met? Are there qualities that are equally important? Whatever the case, when appraisal time comes around, the direct reports should be pretty confident about how well they've done. Clear goals and their standards of measurement help remove the dread that some staffers feel about the performance appraisal process.

- As much as possible, ensure the goals provide objectives to achieve the current work and some objectives that build skills for the future.

One way I've found helpful and inclusive when co-developing goals is to have the direct report prepare for the goal-setting meeting by writing brief responses to the following three items.

Direct Report: My Thoughts on My Next Year's Goals

a. What are one to three different ways I'd like to approach my job role that will enable me to grow professionally and contribute to the organization next year?

b. One area of our team (or organization's) work that I am passion about that I'd like to give my energy to is.....

c. One way I can be a better contributor to the team is...

Then, during the goal-setting meeting, integrate the responses into the conversation. This allows you to incorporate some (even if not all) of the direct report's recommended goals. This builds buy-in and helps the staffer feel heard.

2. Cadence of goal checkpoints

A once-a-year frequency for appraising performance is woefully ineffective and can cause untold angst. Staff should not have to guess all year long about how well you believe they are performing. So, establish a rhythm of checkpoints on progress, challenges, and any needed changes related to the goals. This could be part of your one-on-one meetings bi-monthly or quarterly. Such periodic checkpoints provide staff enough time and support to correct any performance that might be falling short as well as celebrate what's going well.

These two-way conversational checkpoints can be informal or a bit more structured. Such a conversation might go like this:

- **Before the conversation:** *Next week, when we talk, let's check in on your progress towards your annual goals. I'm doing this with everyone to ensure people have what they need to succeed. Can you take a look at the goals and have a few comments about where you are and share ideas on how you plan to achieve the goals going forward?*

- **During the meeting:** *Can you update me on where you are on your goals at this point? How do you feel about where you are? What do you feel most proud of so far? If you were to predict your end-of-year appraisal, where do* *you see yourself ending up? Are there specific things you need to do better or differently to achieve your goals? Do you need anything from me?* Then review any action steps that come out of the conversation.

These check-ins demonstrate caring, accountability and support—all motivators for high performance. Then, there should be no surprises or trepidation during the annual review.

3. Aligning recognition with desired performance

Rewards such as pay raises, employee of the year, promotions, bonuses, special assignments, and others are best when bestowed based on your employees achieving agreed-upon results. However, performance systems with their reward strategies have been known to be problematic and invite troublesome staff behavior in pursuit of the best annual ratings. So, think through *what* you are rewarding. Consider traits such as ethics, values and professional standards; emotional maturity, initiative, communication, team effectiveness, and collaboration when recognizing quality performance (perhaps include these type attributes in annual goals under professional development).

I sent the team to Paris! And they're still grumbling. "*I wanted people to be more motivated on their jobs. I offered outstanding benefits and perks, unlimited vacation, and more. Yet, they kept quitting; they were rude and* *confrontational; and their work was poor and unreliable. I paid for the entire team to go to Paris, hoping to motivate them to do better at work. They loved the trip but returned behaving exactly the same."* –small business owner.

The Paris excursion unintentionally incentivized poor behavior and reflected the leader's avoidance of making performance-related decisions. The urgent need to make tough decisions is more acute when the culture has become corrosive and infects others. Expensive incentives will not improve a culture devoid of consequences for poor behavior and low performance.

Provide incentives that showcase the desired performance and values-based behaviors. Use regular and end-of-year affirming acknowledgments. To do this well, pay attention to the types of incentives that have meaning for each of your direct reports.

4. Better appraisal meetings

When the time arrives for the *real* appraisal meetings (those that determine the on-record, official performance ratings), you can make these gatherings effective and satisfying. Your year-round checkpoints, adjustments, and reinforcements set the stage for meaningful year-end meetings.

With year-round practices in place, performance appraisals become predictable, making way for these appraisal sessions to be more future-focused. They become essentially proactive coaching sessions that take a look back then spend most of the time looking toward the next stage of accomplishment. These conversations can be affirming and relationship-enhancing.

Organizations have various methods for conducting the annual review meeting, and some have no prescribed approach. I have found the following to be useful to prepare for these meeting.

a. **Prior to the meeting**, have the direct report 1) note how well they have performed on each objective and the case for their conclusions, and 2) prepare a reflection on the prior year's work successes, challenges, points of pride, and how their work added value to the organization or department.

b. **During the meeting**, be an interested, fully present listener as you would in your other coaching sessions.

Better appraisal meetings are within your span of control, even if there is a general process established by the organization. Plan to conduct these meetings in ways that reduce your team members' foreboding, reflect equity and fairness, and increase confidence and new possibilities for the future.

5. Performance-based transitions: up, over or out

With effective leadership practices in place (addressed throughout *The Everyday Leader*), there are occasions when transitions are the best way forward. Sometimes, given all your effort to lead well for the good of the organization and staffer, you will ask: *Is it time to move on with this person? Where can they better use their talents? How can I help them win?*

Winning means knowing when and how to guide a team member to better uses of their talents—whether moving up, over or out. This could involve supporting a high performer in getting to their next, elevated job role (a promotion within or elsewhere) rather than stagnate and underuse their talents by keeping them in the same role. It might mean shifting some of a direct report's job functions to better match their valued skills. And it can require dismissal—when a direct report fails to change and grow (after development efforts conclude with little return on investments to help them succeed in their job).

Common reasons for dismissals: There is generally a small set of causes for discharging a direct report. They are:

1) skillset proved incompatible with the job requirements, and investments in development did not yield needed results

2) despite efforts to create a healthy, supportive culture, individual became deeply toxic with an adverse impact on others

3) one or more legal and ethical infractions, such as theft, drug or narcotics use, falsifying resumes, harassment

4) organizational realignments resulted in job elimination

5) individual has personal or emotional challenges that make them incapable of doing their jobs—a situation beyond your scope to resolve. These should be referred to human resources for professional support and the best way forward.

Effects of avoidance: Retaining a staffer who is in a state of chronic poor performance can have a range of negative impacts. Such situations demotivate higher performers, cause the team to fall short on its goals, the individual in question is demoralized or feels mistreated, the work culture further sours, and your credibility suffers for failure to address the issues.

Make the tough decisions in these rare cases, and do your best, professional job of transitioning non-performers. Be prepared, ensure their privacy, preserve the person's dignity as much as possible, and advise them of any supports the organization will provide as they transition out and on.

A hard lesson. *"One of my most challenging experiences was when one individual had some moral/character challenges that created a toxic environment for all of the staff. It was a huge lesson I've carried with me throughout my career. The lesson was that if an individual has character issues, such as chronic dishonesty when asked a direct question or always finding fault they will not do well in the team environment I create. Another lesson in this was that when I had the opportunity to release this person, my fears of how I might be seen stopped me from acting. I allowed myself to be held hostage by an employee who I thought had all the knowledge, important contacts and relationships was a mistake, that nearly destroyed the team. I have not hesitated to release someone toxic since, which has paid off and allowed for teams to develop more quickly."* –interviewee, nonprofit CEO

Closing the chapter with my story: The point in sharing the brief story that follows is to emphasize it takes time and intention to be effective leading others.

In my early years, like many social sector leaders, I spewed out such wistful adages as "we value people above all else. Our employees are our first customers." Nonetheless, I had the unfortunate opportunity to terminate the employment of more people than I'd wished for.

As I evolved as a leader, I spent more thought and effort aligning each new hire with the skills and attributes needed for the job. Then I did my best to apply humane, focused approaches to closing any gaps in skills and behaviors for success in the job. Much of this applied learning is reflected in the Five Keys addressed in this part of The Everyday Leader.

My termination history, fortunately, faded to almost zero, having learned how to lead in a way that made it possible for these talented people to perform at a high level. And, when needed, I was able to facilitate a staffer's transition to a more compatible role respectfully and with their human decency intact—and mostly through their choosing and ability to read the signs all around them.

You've made it through examining the Five Keys for masterfully leading others. Take a moment to celebrate your role in helping your team and the organization PERFORM well. Then, complete this final activity related to the PERFORM key.

A reflection on the PERFORM key: Think through the topics covered in this chapter on evoking and inspiring performance. Jot down a few things that you will integrate into how you cultivate your team's high performance.

☑ Actions I will take....

____

____

____

____

☑ Attitudes I will shift...

____

____

____

____

☑ Better outcomes I expect....

____

____

____

____

Chapter 14, The Perform Key closes **Part Three, Know and Grow Your People**. Spend time periodically reviewing some of the ideas and expanding your knowledge of some of the topics. *The Everyday Leader* set out to provide a broad stroke on getting really good at leading people. Hopefully, you will experience and celebrate your growth year after year.

Wrap Up: Ongoing Leading, Ongoing Growth

This wraps up *The Everyday Leader*. This collection of thoughts and strategies are presented to you as a *people-leader* in support of your continuing leadership progression in an ever-fluctuating work context. Hopefully, you've bookmarked some pages with ideas that resonated and will refresh yourself on those nuggets at the right moments on your journey.

Undoubtedly, there are high-talent people who prefer not to have direct reports, instead remaining as stellar individual contributors. Others of us take on leadership roles that require people to report to us, follow us, and be influenced by us. Let us take this responsibility seriously, then do our best for those who entrust so much of their livelihood to us.

Embrace a bit of humility in your leadership role since our accounting of people's performance has wide-ranging implications. These people MUST report to us, like it or not. It's built into the infrastructure of most organizations. Only on a tiny percentage of occasions do employees get the option to be *freed* from reporting to a leader who doesn't work well for them. That's the case for writing this book—to support each of us in becoming the best leaders we can by improving our skills and attitudes for effectiveness.

The three major sections of *The Everyday Leader* were designed to enhance your knowledge, skills and thinking about 1) the nature of the contemporary work environment; it has changed, and many leaders have not. You can and should. 2) building self-awareness and self-efficacy as a person and a leader. There are many payoffs, one of which is that when you grow, everyone around you grows too, especially your direct reports, and 3) applying five keys to leading your team exceptionally well by attending to their growth, development and performance.

The book was not meant to be all-inclusive; it is intended to be comprehensive enough to start you on your journey. Hopefully, you will expand your knowledge, explore some of the topics more deeply to increase expertise. Secondly, keep the book within reach so you can return to some of the chapters as your work shifts. Refresh yourself over and over again.

Thank you for reading *The Everyday Leader and* thank you for serving as a leader in ways that enrich lives and communities.

Appendix

Five More Resources

Here are five (5) more resources (or tools) I've used through the years. You may want to adapt them as you grow your *leading others* toolset. These resources are referenced in chapters of *The Everyday Leader*.

Tool Name	Supports chapter...
1. Leader 360° informal interview guide	Chapter 6
2. Sample leader coaching topics	Chapter 8
3. Four quadrant activity for better time allocation	Chapter 10
4. One-on-one coaching meeting guide	Chapter 12
5. Better, transformational offsite tips	Chapter 13

Tool #1: Leader 360° Feedback Questionnaire Guide

This is one low-cost, more intimate 360° feedback process. It can help a leader affirm what's going well, unveil valuable opportunities, and uncover blind areas of consequence. This version focuses on respondents' examining what is working well and the desired future with this leader.

Request six to 12 people to participate in a 30-minute phone interview using the provided questions. Include a combination of people who know the leader from various vantage points (peers, direct reports, supervisor, and [optional] another stakeholder or partner). If a few desired respondents can't do the phone interview, opt to email the questionnaire.

Have leader preview and identify questions they believe a) useful to their growth, 2) unnecessary, and 3) should be added.

Choose from or adapt these questions:

1. What is going very well with (*name*) in their (*job title*) role with the organization (e.g., behaviors or attributes)?

2. What 2-3 strengths do you see (*name*) demonstrating that are making a positive difference for the organization (*or department*)?

3. That said, what suggestions or opportunities might (*name*) not be aware of that's important to their leadership? (Or I suggest [*name*]...)

4. To what extent and how is your and (*name*)'s success linked? How well is (*name*) meeting your needs to enable you to do your job? Is there anything else you need from (*name*) to deliver your best work?

5. In 12-18 months, what do you believe is the greatest impact (*name*) can make related to the organization's (or *department's*) success?

6. What are 1-2 ways YOU can further support (*name*) in their role?

7. **Other:** Is there anything else that you want to add to support (*name*)'s success in their role and contribution to the organization (or team)?

8. Finally, will you provide a rating on some items related to (name)'s leadership qualities? Rate between 1 -5, 5 the highest, 1 is the lowest.

Item: (Name) is....	***Rating***
1. Comfortable with other experts in the room.	
2. Effective with problem solving.	
3. Builds and evokes openness and trust.	
4. Demonstrates strategic (big picture) thinking.	
5. Provides meaningful feedback useful to my growth	
6. Sets clear direction.	
7. Open to and applies feedback from those they lead.	
8. Creates an inspiring environment for their team to do their best work.	
9. Controls emotions and behaviors during stressful times.	
10. Includes diverse voices to inform decision-making	
11. Trusted to have my back and consider my best interest.	
12. A leader who spends most of their time doing work at the level expected of their role.	

What should happen next with the 360°?

- Email the respondents to thank them for their valued input. Let them know it will be combined with others' thoughts, then shared the leader as a brief summary of observations.

- Create a summary report (not more than two pages total) with the key themes and highlights, along with average scores on the rated items. Always begin the report with what is valued by the respondents related to the leader's work and remarks about areas of opportunity.

    - Do not include outlier comments (those from one person that are not themes across the majority of the interviews).

    - Do not include quotes in the summary that would clearly identify the respondent.

- Share with the leader, ask leader to reflect on the observations—what impressions aligned with their own, any points of pride, and surprises.

- Then, ask the leader to identify the most value-adding actions to take based on these and their own observations.

Tool #2: Sample Leadership Coaching Topics

The list below contains common topics/goals leaders address during coaching engagements. This list might help you partner with your coach or help you work with your direct reports as you apply coaching to your supervisory practice. There is space to add any other topics/goals.

---

1. Improve management style with direct reports
2. Identify and magnify my important strengths at work
3. Grow self-awareness; reveal things I should know
4. Improve communication and better handle conflict
5. Think and act with greater creativity and innovation
6. Adapt my style to embrace ambiguity and frequent change
7. Improve stress and well-being to better use my energy
8. Improve effectiveness after a setback
9. Address intergenerational challenges, e.g., styles and expectations
10. Manage stressful work expectations and culture
11. Break down organizational silos
12. Increase level and quality of collaboration
13. Develop and lead with vision and values
14. I need an ongoing partner and confidante to test my thinking.
15. Improve influencing skills
16. Enhance executive demeanor and skills; improve perceptions

---

17. Elevate my leadership attributes for a new role
18. Learn strategies to deal with difficult people
19. Effectively balance my work and home life for better satisfaction
20. Develop ways to overcome resistance to organizational change
21. Better manage the activities and work of my board
22. Redesign the work culture to achieve more
23. Support in rolling out a complex change project
24. Increase interpersonal effectiveness
25. Celebrate/honor staff successes to support, develop and retain
26. Career development: prepare for a next role or expand mine
27. Strengthen a high-performing team
28. Succession planning
29. Get more accomplished, demonstrate results/impact
30. Overcome a known weakness that may affect my work
31. Other:
32. Other:

Tool #3: Four-quadrants: Better Time Allocation

This activity asks you to assess then optimize how you use your time to achieve the best results. Some leaders begin by blocking small time segments to focus on their most important work.

Review the Steven Covey time quadrants below. Then fill in your own quadrants and respond to the questions provided.

	URGENT	NOT URGENT
IMPORTANT	Quadrant #1 **"NECESSITY"** Your Key Action: **"MANAGE"** ***Common Activities*** - Crises - Deadline-driven activities - Medical emergencies - Other "true" emergencies - Pressing problems. - Last minute preparations	Quadrant #2 **"QUALITY & PERSONAL LEADERSHIP"** Your Key Action: **"FOCUS"** ***Common Activities*** - Preparation and planning - Values clarification - Empowerment - Relationship-building - True recreation
NOT IMPORTANT	Quadrant #3 **"DECEPTION"** Your Key Action: **"USE CAUTION** or **AVOID"** ***Common Activities*** - Meeting other people's priorities and expectations - Frequent interruptions: - Most emails, some calls - Urgency masquerading as importance	Quadrant #4 **"WASTE"** Your Key Action: **"AVOID"** ***Common Activities*** - Escapist activities - Mindless tv-watching - Busywork - Junk mail - Some emails - Some calls

Adapted from Stephen Covey's "First Things First" - Covey Leadership Center, Inc. © 2003

How are your quadrants?

1. What's in your four boxes? Make notes in the quadrants.

2. What percentage of your time are you spending in each box? Place a percentage in each box.

3. In which areas do you need to spend more time? Are you spending enough time on work that builds the organizational capacity?

4. In which quadrant(s) do you need to spend less time?

1 Important and Urgent	**2 Important, Not Urgent**
3 Not important and Urgent	4 Not important and not urgent

5. What actions will you take to spend more time in the most important quadrants? (eliminate, delegate, stop, start, etc.)

1.
2.

Tool #4: One-on-one Coaching Meeting Guide

Here's an example of an adaptable coaching-style meeting with each direct report. It is best for 45–60-minute meetings. This allows you to work with your staff to look back and forward—including relevant updates, problem-solving, and future plans.

Minutes	The Flow (flexible)	Purpose
3	How are things?	A moment to connect and for direct report to be in the present before shifting topics.
5	What's been going well since our last conversation?	To learn of and affirm what's working well in their work
3	What's the most important things we should talk about today?	The direct report's agenda and priority topics (to address during this session)
10	Can you check in on the actions you agreed to take the last time we talked?	To check accountability for anything the direct report committed to do during your last meeting
15	How about looking at the topics you have?	This allows direct report to have your ear and support as they address pressing work or career issues.
10	Any project/work updates to share?	This should cover perceptions of performance.
3	What will you do to move forward?	These are the direct reports action steps in response to goals and challenges they are pursuing

5	Closing: Updates and support. Are there things you'd like from me to support you as you move forward? I have a few quick updates before we end.	This shows the partnership role you play with your direct reports. You can also suggest a way to support and check if that would be useful to them. Share few quick updates or reminders.

Tool #5: Tips for better, transformational off-sites

Staff retreats (off-sites) can be valuable when these extended, dedicated, no-distraction events are well planned. These are high-cost events that should be well-planned with the intent on accelerating both the team's work performance and their collaborative connections.

Off-sites are relaxed and enjoyable work-related events. To make the most of them, here are some considerations for planning to increase a good return on the investment of the organization and the participants.

Preparation Areas[42]	Questions to consider in advance
Purpose. The most important item to address because it informs the rest of the planning and helps to determine whether retreat was effective. Clarify this first.	WHY are we having the retreat? What is our clear, succinct purpose statement? What do we want to accomplish? What's the value that makes it worth the investment? What do we want people to FEEL, KNOW, and DO as a result?
Products. The most important results, outputs, deliverables that are accomplished by the end of the retreat	What will have happened that tells us the retreat was successful? What are the specific outputs we will have by the end of the day? What will participants know, feel, have and do by the end?

[42] The six Ps of preparation themes are adapted from lead-strat.org.

People. The participants and their roles	Do we have the right people, those who can contribute to the purpose and goals? What ways can we engage the participants in planning, pre-thinking and execution of the retreat? How will we get the most out of the number of people we have?
Possible Issues. This identifies, in advance, the possible issues that could interfere with achieving the purpose and leaving with the products. Once identified, determine how to mitigate those issues.	Are there processes, cultural habits, logistics, or people concerns that could derail the retreat if not addressed during planning? How do we plan for that to achieve our goals?
Process* The agenda, its topic, flow, timeframes, and engagement activities	What's the best use of the time we have allotted? How do we structure the flow of the day to achieve our purpose and leave with our products? How do we make the day one that everyone will feel was a great investment of time? Have we embedded activities that foster new learning, build spirit of team, and engage everyone meaningfully? Have we included some participants in leading parts of the retreat? Have we kept the agenda limited to a small set of topics so we can get the most from them?
Place. The location, amenities and set up	Is the location conducive to what we are trying to accomplish? What tools, materials do we need on hand? How should the room be arranged? Are there other spaces at the site that would contribute to meeting our goals?

Involve Participants Before the Retreat

Participants should be involved in planning and getting ready for the offsite sessions. This creates buy-in and captures their attention early. It can also be a time-saver.

Gather participants input: Find a simple method to ask participants' thoughts on some of the questions in the table above. This helps the leader or planning team establish the priority items, goals and activities.

Sample survey questions:

1. What are your suggestions on what you'd like us to accomplish during the retreat?
2. What would need to happen to cause you to say the retreat was successful?
3. What do you want to make sure doesn't happen?
4. What do you want us to consider as outputs (or outcomes) from the retreat?
5. What should we be sure to include on the retreat agenda?
6. What elements of the retreat are most important to you?

Prepare participants: What can the participants do in advance to prepare them to engage meaningfully in the most important retreat topics? Is there an article to read, a video to view, a worksheet to complete, someone to interview prior to the session that helps them get ready?

About the Author

Lindiwe Stovall Lester spent 40 years doing *the people work* described in *The Everyday Leader*, and she's been a partner to many others to become masterful at it. She retired as a national nonprofit senior leadership consultant. Currently, as the founder and president of Tap In Consulting, she partners with clients as a certified executive coach, team and organizational strategy facilitator, and human performance consultant.

She is keen on mentoring the generations of leaders that follow hers, from the high school years onward. A lifelong learner, Lindiwe makes sure she includes people representing multiple generations in her circle to both enliven her understanding and stay abreast of changes and trends. A committed advocate for access and inclusion, Ms. Lester remains involved in coaching and mentoring current and emerging leaders-of-color.

Lindiwe holds both master's and post-master's degrees in instructional and human performance systems. Additionally, she is certified in executive coaching, social and emotional intelligence coaching, and DISC behavior analytics.

Her family and friends, writing, art, and travel assume big spaces in her heart and schedule.

Acknowledgements

I extend gratitude to the special communities throughout my adult years that provided the experiences, support, challenge and inspiration for me to lead and help others do the same. I mention in the book that we sometimes *fall into leadership*. That was the case in my early adult life; thanks to those who just thought I could do it, those who somehow grew because I was there, and those who functioned as experiment participants while I developed the skills, demeanor and commitment to become an effective leader.

Specifically, I acknowledge my Pan African Orthodox Christian Church community during my early years. Together, we built an outreach ministry committed to transforming people and communities. With you, I learned about group dynamics, onboarding, discipline, accountability, leadership, change management, and more while embracing a philosophy around untapping the vast, mostly unrealized potential of people.

Regarding my second two decades as a nonprofit leader, I am gratified I was afforded the autonomy to lead, learn, innovate, structure, think, restructure, hire, release, then segue into hiring better, developing, coaching, engaging, and empowering people to achieve at elevated levels. For that, I extend thanks to the Detroit YMCA and YMCA of the USA.

I am also indebted to my coaching and consulting partner-clients. These pages emerged because you trusted me with your goals, inner lives, thoughts and fascinating stories. Working with you has been confirmative of my espoused belief that people really can keep growing, regardless of age or experience, and are not in a fixed state of being. Special thanks to Kevin Grant, once a direct report and now a colleague. His ears are always open, and he's an enthusiastic cheerleader who puts into action the practices we've talked about for over a decade.

There's no denying the immeasurable value of the support I received from my partners for life. My husband, Sondai, has been there as a thinking companion, lifting out stories that I'd passed over, and our daughter Noni, a partner in the people work, tested, refined and contemporized my words and ideas.

I acknowledge my good friends Dr. Cynthia Ward, Jackie Gordon, and Dr. Diane Jackson. You helped me make meaning of my experiences and contributed some of yours to this effort.

One final person, who helped build my identity as a coach, was Dr. Larry Kameya. You told me I was *naturally* a coach years before I took that identity seriously, though I remembered. It's amazing how a singular remark can change everything!

Made in the USA
Middletown, DE
02 March 2022

61947718R00163